THE BAPTIST FAITH AND MESSAGE

Herschel H. Hobbs

Convention Press
Nashville, Tennessee

CONTENTS

The Baptist Faith & Message

FOREWORD

The Many Sides of Greatness: A Tribute to Herschel Hobbs

Few men are born with so many talents. Fewer still are those people who learn how to use the skills God in His grace has provided them. Herschel Hobbs, as much as any man I know, mastered the art of being and doing both.

Name the fields in which he achieved special recognition. He was scholar, teacher, writer, radio preacher, administrator, negotiator, peacemaker, citizen, presiding officer, theologian, organizer, and most of all, a pastor.

Dr. Hobbs lived what he taught and wrote, giving his hearers and readers a role model as well as a source of authority. What he presented was always with conviction and clarity and in my 63 years of close association with him, I saw him under every trying situation imaginable and yet he was never anything less than a perfect gentleman. He was a man of solution, not retribution. It was an art he used well.

I saw him in tense situations in his roles of leadership as head of strategic committees or when presiding over the main body as president of the Southern Baptist Convention. I have seen people try to take advantage of him, try to throw him off base or upset him. Lesser men might have come away from such experiences disillusioned and even embittered, but not Herschel. He might have been disappointed at times, but he was totally forgiving of any who had misjudged him or treated him wrongly.

When a revision in the strategic Baptist Faith and Message statement was needed, he was made chairman and served well and objectively as the convention voted points of revision step-by-step. When the Peace Committee was named, he was one of the ones considered indispensable if the committee was to be helpful. When problems of doctrinal or polity arose, his opinions were always considered most valuable. When the Life and Work Series of Sunday School lessons was being developed, he was the one man on the horizon who met all the requirements needed to produce a quarterly publication in book form containing profound truths of Scripture presented in the simple language of the man in the streets.

Through his long life Herschel Hobbs used every skill God gave him in a magnificent way. He recognized these gifts as being divinely given and spent his life honoring the One who in grace gave them. In addition to his abilities, he demonstrated the highest degree of commitment to his Lord. He lived a unique life and made almost unlimited contributions to his day and generation. Through his writings his influence will live on among us for a long time to come.

James L. Sullivan

INTRODUCTION

My little book *The Baptist Faith and Message* was published in 1971. There was not another printing until 1979. Beginning that year, there has been a new printing each year, indicating that more Southern Baptists are studying the basics of our faith and message.

Therefore, it was a happy choice to revise the 1971 edition for the Southern Baptist Convention's 1997 Baptist Doctrine Study. In no sense does this involve a change in the doctrines themselves. It is simply to update developments concerning the articles of faith.

For instance, what is the origin of the words about the Bible: "It has God for its author, salvation for its end, and truth, without any mixture of error, for its matter"?

In 1969 the New Orleans Convention voted down a motion to require all its agencies to adopt The Baptist Faith and Message as their statement of faith. Yet following that, each Southern Baptist agency has done so voluntarily. Three seminaries—Southwestern, Midwestern, and Golden Gate—use this statement as the articles of faith each faculty member signs. The other three seminaries place it alongside the articles to be signed as their statement of faith. Similar refusals through the years to change a single word or phrase in The Baptist Faith and Message speak to its wide acceptance among our people.

Throughout this book, frequent quotations from The Baptist Faith and Message statement of faith are made without footnotes. The reader may wish to refer to the section of the statement which is provided at the beginning of each chapter.

It would be well if each church would present a copy of this book to every new member so that they may know that Southern Baptists as a people remain true to "the faith … once delivered unto the saints" (Jude 3).

Herschel H. Hobbs
3 John 2

The Baptist Faith & Message

PREAMBLE

The 1962 session of the Southern Baptist Convention, meeting in San Francisco, California, adopted the following motion.

"Since the report of the Committee on Statement of Baptist Faith and Message was adopted in 1925, there have been various statements from time to time which have been made, but no overall statement which might be helpful at this time as suggested in Section 2 of that report, or introductory statement which might be used as an interpretation of the 1925 Statement.

"We recommend, therefore, that the president of this Convention be requested to call a meeting of the men now serving as presidents of the various state Conventions that would qualify as a member of the Southern Baptist Convention committee under Bylaw 18 to present to the Convention in Kansas City some similar statement which shall serve as information to the churches, and which may serve as guidelines to the various agencies of the Southern Baptist Convention."

Your committee thus constituted begs leave to present its report as follows:

Throughout its work your committee has been conscious of the contribution made by the statement of "The Baptist Faith and Message" adopted by the Southern Baptist Convention in 1925. It quotes with approval its affirmation that "Christianity is supernatural in its origin and history. We repudiate every theory of religion which denies the supernatural elements in our faith."

Furthermore, it concurs in the introductory "statement of the historic Baptist conception of the nature and function of confessions of faith in our religious and denominational life." It is, therefore, quoted in full as part of this report to the Convention.

"(1) That they constitute a consensus of opinion of some Baptist body, large or small, for the general instruction and guidance of our own people and others concerning those articles of the Christian faith which are most surely held among us. They are not intended to add anything to the simple conditions of salvation revealed in the New Testament, viz., repentance towards God and faith in Jesus Christ as Savior and Lord.

"(2) That we do not regard them as complete statements of our faith, having any quality of finality or infallibility. As in the past so in the future Baptists should hold themselves free to revise their statements of faith as may seem to them wise and expedient at any time.

"(3) That any group of Baptists, large or small have the inherent right to draw up for themselves and publish to the world a confession of their faith whenever they may think it advisable to do so.

The Baptist Faith & Message

"(4) That the sole authority for faith and practice among Baptists is the Scriptures of the Old and New Testaments. Confessions are only guides in interpretation, having no authority over the conscience.

"(5) That they are statements of religious convictions, drawn from the Scriptures, and are not to be used to hamper freedom of thought or investigation in other realms of life."

The 1925 Statement recommended "the New Hampshire Confession of Faith, revised at certain points, and with some additional articles growing out of certain needs...." Your present committee has adopted the same pattern. It has sought to build upon the structure of the 1925 statement, keeping in mind the "certain needs" of our generation. At times it has reproduced sections of the Statement without change. In other instances it has substituted words for clarity or added sentences for emphasis. At certain points it has combined articles, with minor changes in wording, to endeavor to relate certain doctrines to each other. In still others—e.g., "God" and "Salvation"—it has sought to bring together certain truths contained throughout the 1925 Statement in order to relate them more clearly and concisely. In no case has it sought to delete from or to add to the basic contents of the 1925 Statement.

Baptists are a people who profess a living faith. This faith is rooted and grounded in Jesus Christ who is "the same yesterday, and today, and for ever." Therefore, the sole authority for faith and practice among Baptists is Jesus Christ whose will is revealed in the Holy Scriptures.

A living faith must experience a growing understanding of truth and must be continually interpreted and related to the needs of each new generation. Throughout their history Baptist bodies, both large and small, have issued statements of faith which comprise a consensus of their beliefs. Such statements have never been regarded as complete, infallible statements of faith, nor as official creeds carrying mandatory authority. Thus this generation of Southern Baptists is in historic succession of intent and purpose as it endeavors to state for its time and theological climate those articles of the Christian faith which are most surely held among us.

Baptists emphasize the soul's competency before God, freedom in religion, and the priesthood of the believer. However, this emphasis should not be interpreted to mean that there is an absence of certain definite doctrines that Baptists believe, cherish, and with which they have been and are now closely identified.

It is the purpose of this statement of faith and message to set forth certain teachings which we believe.

Herschel H. Hobbs
Chairman

Howard M. Reaves	Ed. J. Packwood	C. Z. Holland
W. B. Timberlake	C. V. Koons	Malcolm B. Knight
Dick H. Hall, Jr	Charles R. Walker	Walter R. Davis
Garth Pybas	V. C. Kruschwitz	Luther B. Hall
Robert Woodward	Douglas Hudgins	Paul Weber, Jr.
R. A. Long	Nane Starnes	C. Hoge Hockensmith
Hugh R. Bumpas	David G. Anderson	E. Warren Rust
James H. Landes	R. P. Downey	

Dr. Herschel H. Hobbs, chairman of the committee that recommended *The Baptist Faith and Message* approved by the Southern Baptist Convention in 1963 produced this commentary to explain and illuminate that confession of faith.

The Southern Baptist Convention has adopted two subsequent revisions to the *The Baptist Faith and Message*; the first on June 9, 1998, which added Article XVIII, on "The Family," and the second, full revision, adopted on June 14, 2000.

FOUNDATIONS
OF THE FAITH

THE ROCK WHENCE WE ARE HEWN
THE SCRIPTURES

THE ROCK
WHENCE WE ARE HEWN

"Look unto the rock whence ye are hewn," exhorted Isaiah (51:1). It was his call for Judah to consider Abraham, the forefather of the Hebrew people, and his place in God's redemptive purpose. For his place in that purpose should govern theirs. In effect, the prophet challenged them to fix their eyes on the basic principle which should guide them in their relationship to God.

This call suggests the vital need for Baptists to focus their hearts and minds on the underlying principle which characterizes their faith. Only in doing so shall they understand themselves and their relationship to each other in their faith and message.

That Baptists believe certain things definitely is quite evident. The body of this volume will be dedicated to an examination of these beliefs. It is equally evident, however, that the very freedom so dear to every Baptist heart means that there will be differences in details in the expression of their beliefs. What shall be the attitude of one Baptist toward another with regard to these differences? The answer to the question is found in this basic principle which underlies the faith of Baptists. Unless this principle is recognized and practiced, the result is chaos. But if Baptists adhere to this principle they will be able to edify one another in Christian love.

Distinctive Belief

What is the distinctive belief held by Baptists? How may one state this undergirding principle which through the centuries has produced their unity in diversity?

Many suggested answers may be forthcoming. Perhaps to many non-Baptists it might seem to be baptism by immersion and so-called "closed communion." Even among Baptists themselves one may hear varying opinions: the authority of the Bible, the deity and lordship of Jesus Christ, or any number of the more evident beliefs held tenaciously by them. But as vital as these doctrines are in Baptist faith, none of them is principal. Indeed, in the various debates over different articles of faith one fears that this principle is often forgotten, which makes it all the more necessary that this study should begin with it.

Many years ago E. Y. Mullins wrote a book entitled *The Axioms of Religion*. In chapter 3 he discussed "The Historical Significance of the Baptists." He raised the question as to "their distinctive contribution to the religious life and thought of mankind." Pursuing the answer to this question, he discussed such topics as soul freedom, separation of church and state, believer's baptism, regenerated church membership, and the priesthood of believers. Certainly each of these strikes a resounding note in every Baptist heart. However, Mullins concluded that none of these constitute the distinctive belief of Baptists. Some of these are held by other groups.

What then is this distinctive belief? It is "the competency of the soul in religion." Mullins hastened to point out that "this means a competency under God, not a competency in the sense of human self-sufficiency. There is no reference here to the question of sin and human ability in the moral and theological sense, nor in the sense of independence of the Scriptures."[1]

Mullins declares this to be a New Testament principle. Certainly it finds its clearest expression there. However, the principle itself is evident from the beginning of the Old Testament. It is rooted in the nature of both God and humans. God is the infinite, supreme Person. He created people in His likeness. Thus humans are endowed with understanding and the privilege of choice. Persons are not puppets. God does not coerce humans against their wills. People are free to choose, but are responsible for their choices. However, their ultimate responsibility is to God, not to other humans. This principle runs throughout the Old Testament in God's dealings with humans.

However, this principle finds its fullest expression in the New Testament. It involves the very essence of people's relation to God as taught by Jesus Christ. The entire Bible entails God's revelation of Himself and people's ability to receive, understand, and respond to the revelation. For the Christian it involves the presence of the indwelling Christ through the person of the Holy Spirit who guides believers into all spiritual truth.

Personal Learning Activity 1

Can you recall from the Bible one or more examples of God revealing Himself to an individual? What were the ways He did this? What impact did the revelation have on those involved?

_____

_____

_____

_____

The principle of soul competency in religion is both exclusive and inclusive. It excludes all human interference in religion such as episcopacy, infant baptism, religious proxy, and governmental authority in religion. "Religion is a personal matter between the soul and God."

But it includes all elements of true faith. Out of this principle flow all other elements of Baptist belief such as belief in God in His triune revelation, authority of the Scriptures, baptism, regenerated church membership, local church autonomy, priesthood of believers, social action (both corporate and individual), soul freedom, and the separation of church and state.

The competency of the soul in religion is the source of such beliefs. Mullins shows this by listing six axioms of religion.

1. The theological axiom: The holy and loving God has a right to be sovereign.
2. The religious axiom: All souls have an equal right to direct access to God.
3. The ecclesiastical axiom: All believers have a right to equal privileges in the church.
4. The moral axiom: To be responsible man must be free.
5. The religio-civic axiom: A free Church in a free State.
6. The social axiom: Love your neighbor as yourself.[2]

Because of their insistence upon the competency of the soul in religion, the charge of narrow-mindedness in religion is a strange sound to Baptist ears. It is true that they hold to certain specific beliefs. They insist upon the lordship of Jesus Christ and the authority of the Scriptures. But they also insist that every man shall be free to decide for himself in matters of religion. Baptists have ever been the champions of soul freedom, not for themselves alone but for all men. Thus it is that Baptists believe that a person has the right to be a Baptist, Methodist, Presbyterian, Roman Catholic, Jew, infidel, atheist, or whatever he chooses to be. Baptists believe that they are under divine compulsion to preach to all men the gospel as they understand it. But they endeavor to win men by persuasion through the power of the Holy Spirit, not through coercion of any kind.

So in reality Baptists are the most broad-minded of all people in religion. They grant to every man the right that he shall be free to believe as he wants. But they insist upon the same right for themselves. The moment that a Baptist seeks to coerce another person—even another Baptist—in matters of religion, he violates the basic belief of Baptists.

This does not mean that Baptists believe that one can believe just anything and be a Christian or a Baptist. The competency of the soul in religion entails the authority of the Scriptures and the lordship of Jesus Christ. The priesthood of believers grants to every Christian the right to read and interpret the Scriptures as led by the Holy Spirit. But said interpretation must be in harmony with the overall teachings of the Bible. And it must adhere to the revelation of God in Jesus Christ, for the Holy Spirit neither contradicts Himself nor denies God's revelation in His Son.

Now according to non-Baptists, Baptists have a good record with respect to the competency of the soul in religion. But what about the record among Baptists themselves? Recognizing that there are limits beyond which one cannot go and still claim to be a Christian or a Baptist, what about detailed items within the larger framework of the faith generally held by Baptists? Should not the principle of soul competency apply there also?

Even to the casual observer, it is evident that all Baptists do not dot every "i" and cross every "t" in exactly the same way. There is no such thing as "the Baptist faith" or "the historic Baptist faith." These phrases imply a creedal faith, something which Baptists have always avoided. There are certain basic things generally held by Baptists today as through past years. But underlying all of them has been the principle of soul competency in religion.

This fact is inherent in the principle of the priesthood of believers. It is not surprising, therefore, that Baptists should have their differences. The amazing thing is that there are so few. But what should be their attitude where such differences do exist? So long as these differences do not deny the authority of the Scriptures or the lordship of Jesus Christ, they should be resolved in Christian love. Each person should speak the truth as he or she sees it—in love. And each person should grant that right to the other.

For instance, Genesis 1 tells of God's creative work. It relates that this took place in six days. One Baptist sees this as six twenty-four-hour days. Another sees it as involving time periods of undetermined lengths. Should one try to force his or her belief on the other? Or should they have a divided fellowship because of honest differences of opinion? Both agree that "in the beginning God created the heaven and the earth" (Gen 1:1). But should either person presume to know how God did it?

The fact is that the Bible does not say dogmatically how long the creative period lasted. The Hebrew word for "day" (yom), like the English word, may mean any number of things: twenty-four hours, a generation, an era, or an indefinite period of time. Since the Holy Spirit inspired the writing of Genesis 1, it must be concluded that He did not spell out this detail. Had He said "a twenty-four-hour day" or "an indefinite period of time," that would settle it. But since He did not do so, the time element is not a vital point in faith.

So long as two Baptists agree at this point, there should be no grounds for dispute between them. Each should solve the apparent problem—by adhering to the principle of the competency of the soul in religion. If there is any judging to be done, it is God's responsibility, not people's.

At times one hears the prediction that Southern Baptists are about to divide over their faith. In this writer's judgment this is most unlikely. Baptists have always agreed on basics but have had their differences on details. This is because they have a living faith rather than a creedal one. The tensions created by these differences have kept their faith vibrant. In all likelihood the only thing that would divide Southern Baptists with regard to their faith would be for one group—to the right or left of center or even in the center—to attempt to force upon others a creedal faith. So long as they hold to the competency of the soul in religion they will remain as one body in the faith. The very differences which disturb some will serve as counterbalances between extremes with the vast majority remaining in between as always.

"The Baptist Faith and Message" of Southern Baptists is based upon the competency of the soul in religion. Those who drew up the original statement in 1924-25 were careful to safeguard the individual conscience. The committee which revised it in 1962-63 retained this safeguard. The preamble clearly states "that the sole authority for faith and practice among Baptists is the Scriptures of the Old and New Testaments. Confessions are only guides in interpretation, having no authority over the conscience… and are not to be used to hamper freedom of thought or investigation in other realms of life." Further, "such statements have never been regarded as complete, infallible statements of faith, nor as official creeds carrying mandatory authority."

It should be noted that these statements are as much a part of the overall statement adopted in 1963 as are the various elements of faith found in the body of it. If this be denied or ignored, then the statement becomes a creed. Without this safeguard to the individual conscience it is highly doubtful that the Southern Baptist Convention would have voted its approval. If the Convention does not bind the individual conscience, neither should any group or any person within its fellowship endeavor to do so. Whatever the problems which may arise, Baptists must continue to hold to their basic and distinct principle of the competency of the soul in religion. For this is the rock whence they are hewn.

Confessions of Faith

At this point it will be well to look briefly at the Baptist practice of drawing up confessions of faith. In doing so, a word is in order regarding "The Baptist Faith and Message."

Baptists have always shied away from anything that resembled a creed or statement of beliefs to which their people were forced to subscribe. However, it should be noted that through the years various Baptist bodies have drawn up their confessions of faith.[3] Many of these were intended for local use only. Others were designed for a broader use among Baptists. Of special interest to Baptists in America are the Philadelphia Confession (1742) and the New Hampshire Confession (1833). The latter has been widely used by various Baptist bodies in the twentieth century. "In 1925 the Southern Baptist

Convention worked over the [New Hampshire] Confession, adding ten new sections, and published it as an expression of faith generally held by Southern Baptists."[4]

In 1924 the evolution controversy was at white heat, especially concerning the teaching of evolution in the public schools. The Southern Baptist Convention appointed a committee chaired by E. Y. Mullins to draw up a recommended statement of Baptist faith and message. Thus in 1925 the Convention adopted what was called "The Baptist Faith and Message." This statement served in large measure to anchor Southern Baptists to their traditional theological moorings for a generation.

In 1961 a controversy, centered in the interpretation of Genesis, arose among Southern Baptists. It was precipitated by *The Message of Genesis* by Ralph Elliott. Actually this volume was not so much the cause as the occasion for the controversy. For several years many had been saying that Southern Baptists were becoming more liberal in their theological views. Talk was even heard about a possible division in the Convention.

One day shortly before the 1962 Convention session which met in San Francisco, the writer—then the president of the Southern Baptist Convention—Porter Routh, and Albert McClellan were discussing how best to solve the problem. Finally it was agreed that a committee should be appointed to study the 1925 statement and report its findings to the Convention. Subsequently, a recommendation from the Executive Committee to this effect was adopted by the Convention. This committee was composed of the president of the Southern Baptist Convention as chairman and of the presidents of the state conventions. It was felt that such a committee would insure broad coverage of the faith as generally held throughout the Convention territory. The committee was instructed "to present to the Convention in Kansas City some similar statement [to the 1925 statement] which shall serve as information to the churches, and which may serve as guidelines to the various agencies of the Southern Baptist Convention." The action also called for this committee's report to be placed in the hands of the editors of the Baptist state papers and the secretary of the Southern Baptist Convention by March 1 preceding the Convention session in Kansas City.

The committee approached its task prayerfully and carefully. It interpreted its responsibility as containing three alternatives: to draw up a new statement, to recommend a reaffirmation of the 1925 statement, or to recommend a revised form of the 1925 statement. The last course was followed. In so doing the preamble and the basic beliefs of the 1925 statement were followed. Much of that statement remained intact. At certain points words were substituted for clarity, and sentences or paragraphs were added for emphasis. Some articles were combined with minor changes in wording in an effort to relate certain kindred articles. In other cases the committee sought to bring together related truths found throughout the 1925 statement. This 1925 statement was studied word by word. Various points of view held in different sections of the Convention territory were weighed. Agreement was reached on the exact wording of each sentence.

When the first draft of the committee's report was finished, copies were furnished to all seminary professors of the six Southern Baptist seminaries and to those people at the Sunday School Board who were responsible for handling theological writings for that Board. Each of these persons was requested to study the proposed statement. Each of the above units also was asked to study it as a group and to present to the committee any suggested changes. Only minor suggestions for changes were made by all of these people.

The final form of the committee's report was given to the state paper editors and to the Convention secretary. The editors published the statement and wrote editorials about it. Thus Southern Baptists were able to read and study it in advance of the Convention. The report was published in the *Book of Reports* for the Convention session in Kansas City. To enable a comparative study, the 1925 statement and the proposed 1963 statement were printed in parallel columns.

At the Convention itself the proposed new statement was read in its entirety. After a brief debate on one sentence regarding the church—"The New Testament speaks also of the church as the body of Christ which includes all of the redeemed of all the ages"—the report was adopted without changing even a punctuation mark.

This action for the time being largely put to rest the current controversy. From time to time other such matters have arisen. Still others may be expected in the future. Unsuccessful efforts have been made from the floor of the Convention to revise or amend the 1963 statement. But the 1970 Convention in Denver and the 1981 Convention in Los Angeles voted unanimously to reaffirm its acceptance of this statement. Probably some future Convention may feel it advisable to revise the 1963 statement in the light of future needs. If so, it should be done not in a spur-of-the-moment action but after following some procedure similar to that used in 1962-1963.

One may safely say that there is no such thing as an official statement of faith and message among Southern Baptists. But the 1963 statement serves "as information to the churches, and ... as guidelines to the various agencies of the Southern Baptist Convention." Note that it is information and guidelines, not a creed. All of the Convention's agencies and institutions have agreed to use this statement as an expression of their faith. But they have done so voluntarily, not by a vote of the Convention itself. Indeed, the New Orleans (1969) and the Denver (1970) Conventions refused to make acceptance of this statement mandatory upon its institutions and agencies or upon those who work for and/or with them. Thus it remained firm at this point in its belief in the competency of the soul in religion.

No, the 1963 statement of the Baptist faith and message is not a creedal statement. However, the widespread acceptance of it by Southern Baptists demonstrates that, despite their doctrinal differences here and there, they are largely a people united in their faith in the basic body of beliefs commonly held by Baptists.

Unity in Diversity

Holding to the priesthood of all believers differences in interpretation of some doctrines will arise. But there are more basic doctrines which unite us than divide us. Throughout our history, especially in the twentieth century, Southern Baptists have followed what Bill J. Leonard calls the "Grand Compromise" in settling doctrinal problems.[5] This was not a compromise of truth. But holding tenaciously to the basic doctrines, allowances were made for differences of interpretation of certain other ones. This system is an outgrowth of the basic doctrine of soul competency in religion.

Leonard notes that the 1950 Convention in St. Louis departed from it for a win/lose system.[6] If Southern Baptists practice what they profess to believe about soul competency they will prevent doctrinal controversy or soon solve existing ones.

Purpose of this Study

Despite the fact that the 1963 statement of "The Baptist Faith and Message" had been adopted and reaffirmed by the Southern Baptist Convention, it was felt by some that an interpretation of it was needed. Since the writer served as chairman of the committee which prepared and presented it to the Convention, he was requested to attempt such an interpretation. It should be understood, however, that this volume is not an official interpretation. It is the result of one Southern Baptist's effort to set forth his own understanding of the Baptist faith and message.

The chosen procedure is not to attempt a line-by-line interpretation of the various articles in the statement. Rather a chapter will be devoted to each article of belief and the author's discussion of what is involved in it. For purposes of study and comparison, each article dealing with a given belief in the statement will be included at the beginning of given chapters.

Baptists being what they are, perhaps not everyone will agree with every statement made by the author of this volume. This is to be expected, and certainly allowed. But this volume is sent forth with the prayer that it may help in understanding "those articles of the Christian faith which are most surely held among us."

The preamble to the 1963 statement closes with the following words which form a fitting conclusion to this chapter.

Baptists emphasize the soul's competency before God, freedom in religion, and the priesthood of the believer. However, this emphasis should not be interpreted to mean that there is an absence of certain definite doctrines that Baptists believe, cherish, and with which they have been and are now closely identified.

It is the purpose of this statement of faith and message to set forth certain teachings which we believe.

SOME QUESTIONS FOR FURTHER THOUGHT

1. In light of the doctrine of the competency of the soul in religion, how far should one Baptist or a group of Baptists go in seeking to force a particular belief upon another Baptist? upon a non-Baptist?

2. Should orthodoxy be based upon the letter or upon the spirit of the Scriptures? Does unity in diversity undermine or strengthen Baptist faith and fellowship?

3. For a clearer understanding, read through the tract "The Baptist Faith and Message" at one sitting. (See Bibliography.) Check the Scripture references after each section to see how each corresponds to the doctrine involved.

THE SCRIPTURES

The Holy Bible was written by men divinely inspired and is the record of God's revelation of Himself to man. It is a perfect treasure of divine instruction. It has God for its author, salvation for its end, and truth, without any mixture of error, for its matter. It reveals the principles by which God judges us; and therefore is, and will remain to the end of the world, the true center of Christian union, and the supreme standard by which all human conduct, creeds, and religious opinions should be tried. The criterion by which the Bible is to be interpreted is Jesus Christ.

Ex. 24:4; Deut. 4:1–2; 17:19; Josh. 8:34; Ps. 19:7–10; 119:11, 89, 105, 140; Isa. 34:16; 40:8; Jer. 15:16; 36; Matt. 5:17–18; 22:29; Luke 21:33; 24:44–46; John 5:39; 16:13–15; 17:17; Acts 2:16 ff.; 17:11; Rom. 15:4; 16:25–26; 2 Tim. 3:15–17; Heb. 1:1–2; 4:12; 1 Pet. 1:25; 2 Pet. 1:19–21

Baptists have been called a people of the Book. The Book is the Bible. The word *Bible* is the transliteration of the Greek root word *biblos*, which refers to the inner bark of the papyrus plant. Many ancient writings were on rolls of papyrus from which comes the word *paper*. Such a roll was called a *biblion* and contained only one book. The plural of *biblion* is *biblia*, which passed over into Latin as singular and came to mean the Bible.

The Bible is composed of 66 books—39 in the Old Testament and 27 in the New Testament. The Old Testament was written largely in Hebrew, with small portions being in Aramaic. The New Testament was written in Greek, specifically the *Koine* Greek or the common language of the people. Different from classical Greek, through the years it was called "New Testament Greek" as though it were a language prepared by God especially for the writing of the New Testament. The discovery of Greek papyri changed this concept. Papyri refers to that vast number of items—roughly contemporary with the New Testament—which were written about everyday life, such as tax and census records, marriage and divorce contracts, birth and death notices, receipts, grocery bills, and private letters. These were written in the language of the common people. Hence *Koine*, common. Adolph Deissmann discovered that the language of the New Testament was the same as that of the papyri. All but about 50 New Testament words have been found in the papyri and other current writings, throwing a flood of light on the meaning of the New Testament.[1]

The New Testament, therefore, was written in the language of the everyday communication of the people. And it speaks today to the hearts and minds of all who will read it prayerfully and carefully. The same may be said about the Old Testament. For both the Old and New Testaments are the Word of God. And as such, certain things may be said about the Bible.

Isaiah 53

An Inspired Book

"The Baptist Faith and Message" begins its statement on the Scriptures by avowing that "the Holy Bible was written by men divinely inspired and is the record of God's revelation of Himself to man." Thus Baptists believe that the Bible is the inspired written record of God's revelation to men.

In order to comprehend this truth one must consider three words: revelation, illumination, and inspiration. *Revelation* is the process by which God unveils Himself and His will to human messengers. *Illumination* is the Holy Spirit's work as He enlightens the human mind with spiritual understanding in order that persons might grasp the revealed truth. *Inspiration* refers to God's inbreathing into the chosen human messengers through the Holy Spirit, enabling them by divine guidance to deliver or record God's revealed message. In the scriptural sense it means God breathing into His messenger.

As love, God reveals Himself. He does so through nature (Ps. 19:1; Rom. 1:19–20) and the human conscience (Rom. 2:14–15). But revelation in the sense as used here refers to that which finds its fullest expression in Jesus Christ and which is recorded in the Bible. It is a full, complete revelation to be followed by no other of like kind.

Those who received this revelation did not always fully understand it. For instance, David in Psalm 22 and Isaiah in Isaiah 53 wrote more about Calvary than they comprehended. Their great truths were fulfilled in Jesus Christ. And the Holy Spirit illumined the minds of the Gospel writers, Paul, and other New Testament writers so that they might understand and interpret the event for all ages to come. The apostles did not fully comprehend Jesus' words to them. But Jesus promised that the Holy Spirit would help them understand all things that He had said to them. The Spirit still illumines the mind and heart of serious students of God's Word so that they may discover truths hitherto unknown to them.

But even this lack of full understanding on the part of the Old Testament writers is evidence of the Bible's divine inspiration. For they were enabled to look down the centuries and to see things, though dimly, which a natural human mind could not have perceived. This inbreathing applies to both Testaments.

The doctrine of inspiration has led to various theories as to how God inspired His messengers: "(1) the intuition theory, which holds that inspiration is simply a higher development of man's natural insight into truth; (2)

the illumination theory, which views inspiration as simply an intensifying and elevating of the religious perceptions of men; (3) the dictation theory, affirming that the writers were so possessed by the Holy Spirit that they became passive instruments in the hands of God; (4) the dynamical theory, which holds that inspiration is neither natural, partial, nor mechanical, but supernatural, full, and dynamic."[2]

The first of these theories hold that only portions of the Bible are inspired and, therefore, the Bible is subject to human error in the uninspired portions. They are largely rejected by Southern Baptists. One or the other of the last two theories is held by the vast majority of Southern Baptists, some adhering to one and some to the other.

At the Los Angeles Convention some expected an explosion over the nature of Scripture. Hoping to prevent this, I made a motion that we reaffirm our acceptance of the 1963 "Baptist Faith and Message," including all 17 articles.

When it came up for discussion, I quoted 2 Timothy 3:16, All Scripture is God-breathed and is useful for teaching, rebuking, correcting and training in righteousness (2 Tim. 3:16, NIV). I then noted that some held that that which is *Scripture* is inspired, but that all the Bible is not Scripture. But I noted that Paul did not say that. The Greek word for *all* with the definite article means *people or things as a group*. Without the definite article, it means *every single part of the whole*. Since Paul did not use the definite article, he said, "Every single part of the whole of Scripture is God-breathed." Then I added, "A God of truth does not breathe error."

Then Adrian Rogers spoke. He said: "I like what Dr. Hobbs said very much. My only request is that his discussion be printed in the minutes of this Convention." It was unanimously voted that that be done.

That afternoon Dale Moody, noted Greek scholar, said to me, "Herschel, that was a good thing you did this morning." Since then I have not had a Greek professor to challenge that interpretation.

What Strong calls the dictation theory, Mullins calls the verbal theory. It holds that the Holy Spirit selected the very words of the Scriptures and dictated them to the writer. The dynamical theory sees the Holy Spirit as inspiring the thought rather than the exact wording, that the writers were left free to express the truth in their own forms and words, but that in the process the writers were by the Spirit guarded from error. The choice of different words in relating the same event plus the evidence of the writer's own personality in his work strongly support this theory.

However, the verbal and dynamical theories differ only in the method of inspiration. They agree as to the result. Which of these two theories one holds has never been a test of orthodoxy among Southern Baptists. For both groups see all of the Bible as the divinely inspired Word of God.

In whatever way God revealed Himself and inspired men to record that revelation, the result is God's divinely inspired record of His revelation of Himself to men. It should be noted that God's revelation is progressive. This does not indicate His inability to reveal at a given point in time. It refers to man's inability to receive the revelation. Einstein would not have begun with his theory of relativity in teaching a child simple arithmetic. He would have begun with the simpler elements and moved toward his more complex knowledge as the child was able to grasp it. So God began where man was and moved forward in His revelation as man was able to receive it. Thus one finds a greater revelation of God in some parts of the Bible than in others. But all of it is God's revelation. It is the inspired Word of God.

Evidence of divine inspiration is found in the Bible itself. It is seen in its claims about itself. For instance, God spoke to Moses, Joshua, David, and the prophets. "Thus saith the Lord" resounds throughout the prophets. Isaiah began his prophecy with the words, "Hear, O heavens, and give ear, O earth; for the Lord hath spoken" (Isa. 1:2). Likewise, Jeremiah stated, "The word of the Lord came unto me" (Jer. 1:4); "Thus speaketh the Lord God of Israel, saying, Write thee all the words that I have spoken unto thee in a book" (Jer. 30:2). Jesus spoke with the authority of God.

In 1 Corinthians 2:10–13 Paul insisted that his message came to him through the inspiration of the Holy Spirit. (See also Gal. 1:12.) In 2 Timothy 3:16 he declared that "all scripture is given by inspiration of God." Literally, "All scripture is God-breathed." Hester comments, "Holy men divinely breathed upon, or directed, wrote the books which constitute our Bible. As such, they have an authority not true of any other writings."[3]

The writer of 2 Peter 1:20–21 declared that "no prophecy of the scripture is of any private interpretation [origin]. For the prophecy came not in old time by the will of man: but of holy men of God spake as they were moved by the Holy Ghost [Spirit]."

The inspiration of the Bible is also seen in the fulfillment of prophecy. "That it might be fulfilled which was spoken by the prophets" is a phrase found many times in the Gospels. Hundreds of years before some events happened, prophets had prophesied them. Note, for instance, the manner and place of Jesus' birth (Isa. 7:14; Micah 5:2; Matt. 1:22–23; 2:5–6). In Nazareth, Jesus read Isaiah 61:1–2 and said of Himself, "This day is this scripture fulfilled in your ears" (Luke 4:21). In events connected with His trial, death, and resurrection Jesus fulfilled the Old Testament Scriptures concerning Himself (Luke 24:44–46).

Here then were men who lived centuries before Jesus writing with exactness about things pertaining to His life and redemptive mission. No amount of merely human insight and natural heightening of mental perception can explain this. It is explained only by the inspiration of God through His Holy Spirit.

Furthermore, the unity of the Bible attests its inspiration. The Bible has one central theme: God's redemptive purpose. It has one central figure: Christ. It has one central goal: God supreme in a redeemed universe.

The Bible was written over a period of approximately 1,500 years in various places stretching all the way from Babylon to Rome. The human authors included a variety of men in many stations of life—kings, peasants, poets, herdsmen, fishermen, scientists, farmers, priests, pastors, tentmakers, and governors. Among its themes are such content matter as philosophy, poetry, prophecy, theology, history, science, and sociology. Not one of the writers knew that he was writing a part of the Holy Bible. Probably many had no knowledge of what others had written.

Yet when under the guidance of the Holy Spirit the various books were gathered together, they told one complete story. Neither Testament is complete without the other.

Such a phenomenon cannot be explained on the grounds of human reason and purpose. It makes sense only if the Bible is seen as the written revelation of God, the product of divine inspiration, whose authorship, selection, and preservation are all under the guiding hand of the Holy Spirit.

There is no greater evidence of the Bible's inspiration than its message. Its message is unlike that of any other book. The Bible defies comparison with any other literary work of man. The contents of the Apocrypha are as sand compared to the Bible's diamonds and rubies. A comparison with the pseudo-gospels (writings that were not accepted as part of the Canon) of the first two centuries after Christ reveals that the four canonical Gospels tower above them as heaven does the earth.

The Bible contains truth found nowhere else. Human reason may discover certain truths about God. But the revealed truth of the Bible exceeds these so as to defy comparison. One may exhaust the meaning of the contents of other books, but not that of the Bible.

Jesus' Bible was the Old Testament. He regarded it as God's inspired Word. He quoted from it as divine authority. Skeptics may question the inspiration of the Old Testament, but Jesus never did. In *These Things We Believe*, J. Clyde Turner notes that Jesus took two events from the Old Testament and used them to illustrate divine truth: the flood (Matt. 24:38–39) and Jonah and the fish (Matt. 12:40). And Jesus is the final authority!

One final word about the Bible as an inspired book in regard to inspiration and research. Does either of these negate the other? Hardly so. Certainly Luke wrote his Gospel under the inspiration of the Holy Spirit. Yet in Luke 4:1–4, in telling how his Gospel came to be, he clearly said that in the light of previous oral and written records about events in Jesus' life, "it seemed good to me also, having followed all things closely for some time past, to write an orderly account for you" (RSV). The verb forms in Luke 1:1–4 indicate these words were written after he had finished the body of his Gospel. Thus he did not tell what he planned to do but what he had already done.

This passage should calm any fear that reference to source material used by any Bible writer is a denial of divine inspiration. For Luke's writings (Gospel and Acts), in the face of the severest skeptical analysis, have proved their historical accuracy beyond any serious question of doubt. They stand as a bulwark, lending credence to the entire Bible.

Is the Bible a divine Book? Yes. Is the Bible a human Book? Yes. The truth is that it is a divine-human Book. It is divine in that it is the inspired Word of God. It is human in that God chose to record His revelation through men divinely inspired, who were guided in their work and were guarded against error in it.

A Book of Religion

The Bible "is a perfect treasure of divine instruction. It has God for its author, salvation for its end, and truth ... for its matter."

The Bible lays no claim to being a textbook of history, literature, philosophy, psychology, or science. Yet it contains true elements of all these and more. It is not designed as an encyclopedia containing answers to all of man's questions. Yet it answers the vital and ultimate inquiries of the heart, mind, and spirit. It may not tell man all he wants to know, but it does tell him all that he needs to know about his moral and spiritual duty and destiny.

The Bible is primarily a book of religion. Paul said, "All scripture ... is profitable for doctrine [teaching], for reproof, for correction, for instruction [as the training of a child] in righteousness: that the man of God may be perfect [complete and proficient], throughly [thoroughly] furnished [equipped] unto all good works" (2 Tim. 3:16–17).

The Bible speaks of God's redemptive purpose. It reveals how God proposes to bring sinful man back into His fellowship and to use him in His service. From Genesis through Revelation this message runs like a scarlet thread. Its message begins in eternity with the Lamb slain from before the foundation of the world, and ends with the triumphant Lamb on His throne ruling over a redeemed universe. The Bible points forward to Christ, backward to Christ, and again forward to Christ in His glorious return and reign. And it reveals God in the person of the Holy Spirit as He empowers and directs the people of Christ in God's mission of evangelism and missions.

The Bible relates God's redemptive purpose to human history. It shows how He uses people and nations as He pursues His redemptive purpose. And it points to the time at the end of the age when Jesus shall be King of kings and Lord of lords (Rev. 19:16), and when God—Father, Son, and Spirit—shall be all in all (1 Cor. 15:24–28).

The Bible speaks of God's judgment against sin. "It reveals the principles by which God judges us; and therefore is, and will remain to the end of the world ... the supreme standard by which all human conduct, creeds, and religious opinions should be tried."

Throughout the Bible runs this principle of judgment. It depicts God's judgment upon fallen man (Gen. 3:16–19; 4:10–12), an evil race (Gen. 6), nations (Ex. 7–12; Amos), individuals (Num. 20:11–12; 2 Sam. 12:10–12), and His own chosen people (Isa. 5; Matt. 21:33–45).

The Bible tells the story of God's mingled love and wrath (Rom. 1:16–18). God hates sin, but He loves sinners. It shows what God has done to deliver man from judgment (John 3:16–18). But it points to God's final judgment upon unrepentant sinners (Rev. 20:11–15). It also speaks of the judgment of all men (Rom. 14:10)—the saved as to their degree of reward in heaven and the lost as to their degree of punishment in hell (Luke 12:47–48; Rev. 20:12–15).

The Bible is the standard by which God regulates human conduct (2 Tim. 3:16–17). One may discover this truth on almost any page in the Bible. It is seen especially in the Ten Commandments (Ex. 20:1–17). The Sermon on the Mount is the constitution of the kingdom of God, designed not to tell lost men how to be saved, but to teach Christians how to live the redeemed life (John 15; Rom. 6; 12; 1 Cor. 12–14).

The Bible is the true center of Christian union. It reveals the fellowship which believers have in Christ. And if followed absolutely, apart from man-made creeds and practices, it furnishes the one rallying point about which all of God's people may find the unity of faith for which Jesus prayed (John 17:22). *only way to know it is to read it!*

An Authoritative Book

The principle of judgment and guidance suggests the authority of the Scriptures. John P. Newport points out that this authority is both objective and subjective. It is objective in that "it is a divinely inspired and authoritative historical record and interpretation of God's revelation in history." It is subjective in that "the authority of the Bible is not rigid and mechanical. It is a living and pulsating Book which is used by the Holy Spirit to constrain without compelling and to lead without forcing. It is a Book through which the Holy Spirit works to lead men to the living Christ and guide in the Christian way."[4]

All of the Bible is the Word of God. But the Old Testament finds its fulfillment in the New Testament. For this reason Baptists see the note of finality in the New Testament.

To say that the Bible is an authoritative book does not mean that it is authoritative in every field of human thought. It is not an authority in science. It does not claim to be. Keeping in mind that the Bible was written in the popular language of the people, still the phases of creation recorded in Genesis 1 are in harmony with the findings of fields of science related to the

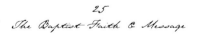

beginning of things, such as geology, botany, and biology.

When one holds the Bible in his hand, he can know that he holds a Book which has been through the fires of the furnace of adverse criticism and has come through with flying colors. As one reads the Bible he does not need to compromise intellect to believe it.

"The Baptist Faith and Message" says that the Bible has "truth, without any mixture of error, for its matter." Whence came the statement "truth, without any mixture of error, for its matter"? Several years before his death, I received a call from Dr. Hugh Wamble, professor of Church History at Midwestern Baptist Theological Seminary. His students had been asking as to the source of that statement. He asked if our committee researched it. I replied in the negative. "It is in the New Hampshire Confession of 1833. The 1925 committee incorporated it in its statement, so we simply retained it."

Fortunately, he researched it. He found a bound volume of letters of John Locke, an English philosopher. A young English minister had written him for advice as to how to have a successful ministry. Locke died in September 1703. This book contained his reply to the young minister, dated in September 1702. He said, "Preach the Bible! For it has God for its author, salvation for its end, and, truth, without any mixture of error, for its matter." These quoted words are in the article on "The Scriptures" in "The Baptist Faith and Message." Coming from a philosopher, not a pastor or theologian, adds strength to the statement.

This, of course, refers to the original manuscripts of its component parts. In St. Louis in 1980 someone objected that he had never seen the original manuscripts. Another replied, "I have never seen Jesus Christ, but I believe in Him." I thought it was a good answer. Serious students of the Scriptures know that, through the years, copyists' errors were made. The Holy Spirit does not guard copyists from such any more than He does typesetters. It should be noted, however, that none of these errors affect the spiritual contents of the Scriptures.

But with the discovery of thousands of manuscripts of the New Testament, most of these errors have been traced to their source and eliminated. Students of the classics are fortunate to have as many as ten or fifteen manuscripts of any given work. Think how fortunate are those who make a critical study of the Scriptures! In textual criticism it is an axiom that an older manuscript is more accurate than a newer one. Some New Testament manuscripts date as far back as the fourth century. It can be safely said that in a comparative study of these documents, scholars probably have been able to determine the exact text of the originals.

In the caves near the Dead Sea have been found the most ancient copies of the Old Testament possessed by modern man. Prior to that discovery, the oldest and most complete Hebrew copies of the Old Testament dated as late as the ninth century. Now portions of the Hebrew text are in hand dating in the first or second centuries B.C. By 1956, about 90 manuscripts of Old Testament books had been identified. These included 13 copies of Deuteronomy, twelve of Isaiah, ten of Psalms, seven of part or all of the twelve prophets, and five of books of the Pentateuch (five books of Moses). Every book of the Hebrew Old Testament is represented except Esther.[5] These Hebrew texts are closely akin to the Septuagint (the Greek translation of the Old Testament).

This within itself has served to substantiate the accuracy of the Septuagint, the version used by most of the New Testament writers. And it has solved a problem in Scripture harmony. Stephen quotes from the Old Testament that seventy-five people went with Jacob into Egypt (Acts 7:14). The Hebrew text which has been followed by English translations states that seventy people went with him (Ex. 1:5). But the Hebrew manuscripts found at Qumran, dating about two centuries before Christ, read seventy-five, the same as the Septuagint used by Stephen. So Stephen (and Luke in Acts) was correct.[6]

The story could be almost endless. One of the most thrilling stories in modern Bible study has been the effects of archaeology in authenticating the Scriptures. There are still problems to be solved. But where seeming discrepancies exist one may rest in faith that they rest upon man's incomplete knowledge, not upon errors in the original manuscripts of the Bible.

Though the word *infallible* does not appear in the Southern Baptist statement, it is well to examine it. The word itself means *incapable* of *erring*. What is the infallibility of the Bible? It is infallible as a book of religion. While Southern Baptists hold to the inerrancy of the Scriptures, their infallibility rests upon the fact that they do what they are designed to do. The Bible, says Mullins, reveals "God's presence among his people using men of varying capacities, who were guided in the selection of a great variety of means for conveying the truth; adapting the means to the end in view and the need to be supplied; employing always the language of common life; sometimes using forms of pictorial representation suitable for a child-race; at others rising to the lofty eloquence of Isaiah and the sublime conceptions of a God infinite in majesty, power, grace, and truth; the whole culminating in the matchless revelation of God in Christ. The Bible then is a book of religion, not of science. As such it has proved hitherto and will continue to prove in the future, man's sufficient and authoritative guide.

"The Bible remains in its place of authority for Christians. It is a vital and living authority, and not a mechanical and ecclesiastical one. It is our authoritative source of information as to the historical revelation of God in Christ. It is regulative of Christian experience and Christian doctrine. It is the instrument of the Holy Spirit in his regenerative and sanctifying influences. … It holds us to the great saving deeds of God in Jesus Christ, the Redeemer and Lord. It is final for us in all the matters of our Christian faith and practice."

The Baptist Faith & Message

Beside each letter of the word Bible below, write a word or phrase beginning with that letter that gives a description of the Bible. How do these descriptive words enhance your view of the Bible?

B _____

I _____

B _____

L _____

E _____

Criterion of Interpretation

"The criterion by which the Bible is to be interpreted is Jesus Christ." The Bible is the written Word about the living Word. Therefore, any interpretation of a given passage must be made in the light of God's revelation in Jesus Christ and His teachings and redemptive work. Indeed, the Bible is its own best interpreter as one discovers the meaning of any particular passage in the light of the whole.

SOME QUESTIONS FOR FURTHER THOUGHT

1. What is the meaning of *inspiration*? What are some of the evidences that the Bible is God's inspired Word?

2. Does research militate against inspiration? Or, does it speak for the accuracy of the Scriptures?

3. Does the Bible speak to your heart? Recall instances when it has proved to be God's Word to you.

BASIC TRUTHS
OF THE FAITH

GOD

MAN

SALVATION

GOD'S PURPOSE OF GRACE

three

GOD

There is one and only one living and true God. He is an intelligent, spiritual, and personal Being, the Creator, Redeemer, Preserver, and Ruler of the universe. God is infinite in holiness and all other perfections. To Him we owe the highest love, reverence, and obedience. The eternal God reveals Himself to us as Father, Son, and Holy Spirit, with distinct personal attributes, but without division of nature, essence, or being.

A. God the Father
God as Father reigns with providential care over His universe, His creatures, and the flow of the stream of human history according to the purposes of His grace. He is all powerful, all loving, and all wise. God is Father in truth to those who become children of God through faith in Jesus Christ. He is fatherly in His attitude toward all men.

Gen 1:1; 2:7; Ex. 3:14; 6:2–3; 15:11 ff.; 20:1 ff.; Lev. 22:2; Deut. 6:4; 32:6; 1 Chron. 29:10; Ps. 19:1–3; Isa. 43:3,15; 64:8; Jer. 10:10; 17:13; Matt. 6:9 ff.; 7:11; 23:9; 28:19; Mark 1:9–11; John 4:24; 5:26; 14:6–13; 17:1–8; Acts 1:7; Rom. 8:14–15; 1 Cor. 8:6; Gal. 4:6; Eph. 4:6; Col. 1:15; 1 Tim. 1:17; Heb. 11:6; 12:9; 1 Pet. 1:17; 1 John 5:7

B. God the Son
Christ is the eternal Son of God. In His incarnation as Jesus Christ He was conceived of the Holy Spirit and born of the virgin Mary. Jesus perfectly revealed and did the will of God, taking upon Himself the demands and necessities of human nature and identifying Himself completely with mankind yet without sin. He honored the divine law by His personal obedience, and in His death on the cross He made provision for the redemption of men from sin. He was raised from the dead with a glorified body and appeared to His disciples as the person who was with them before His crucifixion. He ascended into heaven and is now exalted at the right hand of God where He is the One Mediator, partaking of the nature of God and of man, and in whose Person is effected the reconciliation between God and man. He will return in power and glory to judge the world and to consummate His redemptive mission. He now dwells in all believers as the living and ever present Lord.

Gen. 18:1 ff.; Ps. 2:7 ff.; 110:1 ff.; Isa 7:14; 53; Matt. 1:18–23; 3:17; 8:29; 11:27; 14:33; 16:16,27; 17:5; 27; 28:1–6,19; Mark 1:1; 3:11; Luke 1:35; 4:41; 22:70; 24:46; John 1:1–18,29; 10:30,38; 11:25–27;

12:44–50; 14:7–11; 16:15–16,28; 17:1–5,21–22; 20:1–20,28; Acts 1:9; 2:22–24; 7:55–56; 9:4–5,20; Rom. 1:3–4; 3:23–26; 5:6–21; 8:1–3,34; 10:4; 1 Cor. 1:30; 2:2; 8:6; 15:1–8,24–28; 2 Cor. 5:19–21; Gal. 4:4–5; Eph. 1:20; 3:11; 4:7–10; Phil. 2:5–11; Col. 1:13–22; 2:9; 1 Thess. 4:14–18; 1 Tim. 2:5–6; 3:16; Titus 2:13–14; Heb. 1:1–3; 4:14–15; 7:14–28; 9:12–15,24–28; 12:2; 13:8; 1 Pet. 2:21–25; 3:22; 1 John 1:7–9; 3:2; 4:14–15; 5:9; 2 John 7–9; Rev. 1:13–16; 5:9–14; 12:10–11; 13:8; 19:16

C. God the Holy Spirit

The Holy Spirit is the Spirit of God. He inspired holy men of old to write the Scriptures. Through illumination He enables men to understand truth. He exalts Christ. He convicts of sin, of righteousness and of judgment. He calls men to the Saviour, and effects regeneration. He cultivates Christian character, comforts believers, and bestows the spiritual gifts by which they serve God through His church. He seals the believer unto the day of final redemption. His presence in the Christian is the assurance of God to bring the believer into the fullness of the stature of Christ. He enlightens and empowers the believer and the church in worship, evangelism, and service.

Gen. 1:2; Judg. 14:6; Job 26:13; Ps. 51:11; 139:7 ff.; Isa. 61:1–3; Joel 2:28–32; Matt. 1:18; 3:16; 4:1; 12:28–32; 28:19; Mark 1:10,12; Luke 1:35; 4:1,18–19; 11:13; 12:12; 24:49; John 4:24; 14:16–17,26; 15:26; 16:7–14; Acts 1:8; 2:1–4,38; 4:31; 5:3; 6:3; 7:55; 8:17,39; 10:44; 13:2; 15:28; 16:6; 19:1–6; Rom. 8:9–11,14–16,26–27; 1 Cor. 2:10–14; 3:16; 12:3–11; Gal. 4:6; Eph. 1:13–14; 4:30; 5:18; 1 Thess. 5:19; 1 Tim. 3:16; 4:1; 2 Tim. 1:14; 3:16; Heb. 9:8,14; 2 Pet. 1:21; 1 John 4:13; 5:6–7; Rev. 1:10; 22:17

Baptists believe in "one and only one living and true God." As the supreme personal Spirit, He is the Creator, Preserver, Redeemer, and Ruler of the universe. It is impossible to define God, but it is possible to describe Him.

"God is the supreme personal Spirit; perfect in all his attributes; who is the source, support, and end of the universe; who guides it according to the wise, righteous, and loving purpose revealed in Jesus Christ; who indwells in all things by his Holy Spirit, seeking ever to transform them according to his own will and bring them to the goal of his kingdom."[1]

This description is both comprehensive and practical. It is more than abstract and philosophical. It speaks of what God is in His person and attributes, His relation to the universe, His redemptive purpose in Christ, His work through the Holy Spirit, and the nature and goal of His kingdom. It is distinctly Christian in its concept of God.

Name of God

Elohim.—This is the first name for God found in the Bible (Gen. 1:1). It was the general name for deity and is used for the true God and for pagan gods. The New Testament equivalent is *Theos. El,* which is the short form of *Elohim,* was used in various combinations to denote certain aspects of God's nature. *Adonai.*—Its basic meaning is *Lord.* While sometimes used in the human sense as a term of respect, in the divine sense it carried the thought of personal relationships or that of a helper in time of need. The New Testament equivalent is kurios, Lord. *Jehovah.* The Hebrew word translated *Jehovah* in *The American Standard Version* is *Yahweh.* This was the name most often used for God. It distinguished Israel's God from false gods. The Hebrew form is *Yahweh.* At the burning bush, God revealed Himself to Moses as Jehovah (Ex. 3:14). "I AM THAT I AM." Literally, the Hebrew means "He will be that He will be." Jehovah was beginning to reveal Himself as Redeemer. Through Moses, God was about to redeem Israel out of Egypt. So He revealed Himself as He would then show Himself to be. Thus Jehovah is God's redeeming name. Note that Jesus means *Jehovah is salvation.*

Personal Learning Activity 3

Use the lines provided to write your definition of the names given to God in Scripture.

Elohim _____

_____

_____

Adonai _____

_____

_____

Yahweh _____

_____

Attributes of God

God's attributes are those elements which describe His nature. Mullins lists seven natural and four moral attributes.[2] The seven natural attributes are:

SELF-EXISTENCE.—God exists by reason of what He is in Himself. He is eternal in being (Gen. 1:1; Isa. 57:15).

IMMUTABILITY.—God does not change His character, nature, or purpose. He is active, progressive, free to choose, and He experiences both joy and sorrow. But while changing His methods, He never changes in His nature or purpose (Deut. 4:26–38; Jer. 31:31–34; Matt. 21:33–45; 2 Pet. 2:4–10).

OMNIPRESENCE.—God is present at all times in every part and time of His universe (Ps. 139:7–12). He is limited by neither time nor space, but is a free personal Spirit.

IMMENSITY.—God is superior to space. He is the God of the universe. No human concept can contain Him (Rom. 11:33–36).

ETERNITY.—God has no beginning or end. He is related to events in time, yet He is not confined to time. Past, present, and future are one to Him.

OMNISCIENCE.—God has all knowledge. He knows all things simultaneously. His knowledge is immediate, without the processes of thought, reason, or inference. His foreknowledge of events does not necessarily mean that He predetermined them. He knows the workings of His natural, physical, moral, and spiritual laws which work toward definite ends. Individuals are free to choose in the light of them, but are responsible for their choices. God knows these choices beforehand, but does not predetermine them.

OMNIPOTENCE.—God possesses all power. He can do anything in keeping with His nature and purpose. The only limits to His power are self-imposed. He cannot lie or act contrary to His own laws, character, and purposes. These limitations are evidences of God's power, not of His weakness.

Miracles are acts of God contrary to man's knowledge of natural law, but not contrary to God's knowledge of such, and which He works in accord with His benevolent will and purpose. Thus miracles are not only possible but expected.

The four moral attributes of God are:

HOLINESS.—Holiness connotes God's supreme moral excellence (Isa. 6:3). The word *holy* carries the idea of separation or exaltation. When used of persons or things, it means separated for God's service. Because God is holy, He demands holiness in His people (Lev. 11:44).

RIGHTEOUSNESS.—This is God's self-affirmation on behalf of right as opposed to wrong. As righteous, God cannot ignore or condone evil. Righteousness connotes what God is in His nature, what He demands in man, and what by grace He bestows through Christ upon all who believe in Him (Rom. 3:26; 10:1–13; 2 Cor. 5:19).

TRUTH.—God is the source and ground of all truth. He is the criterion by which all thoughts and acts shall be judged. Truth—whether in science or religion—harmonizes. For all truth is of God. Any error is a departure from God's nature (John 17:17). Jesus answered man's eternal search for truth when He said, "I am the way, the truth, and the life" (John 14:6).

Jesus Christ is the incarnation of truth (John 1:14,17; 14:6). In Him dwells all the treasures of wisdom and knowledge (Col. 2:3).

LOVE.—Love is the attribute which permeates all other of God's attributes. "God is love" (1 John 4:7–10). Love involves absolute loyalty to its object. By it God seeks the complete possession of and the highest good for His creatures.

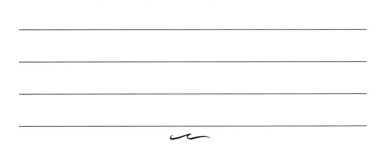

Personal Learning Activity 4
Reread the nine attributes of God. In each one underline key words that reveal the essence of the attribute. How does the last attribute (love) relate to you in a personal way? _____

_____

_____

_____

_____

God a Person

The Bible presents God as the supreme personal Spirit (John 4:24); He possesses all the qualities attributed to personality.

God is one Person. "Hear, O Israel the Lord our God [Elohim] is one Lord [Jehovah]" (Deut. 6:4). This passage denies (1) *dualism* (there are a good and an evil principle of equal power contending for mastery in the universe), (2) *pantheism* (God is identified in everything), and (3) *polytheism* (there are many gods).

Though He is one Person, God reveals Himself as bearing three relationships to man: Father, Son, and Holy Spirit. He is the triune God, three in one. The word *trinity* is not found in the Bible. It was first used by Tertullian in the second century to express the truth taught in the Bible: God the Father (Gen 1:1; Matt. 6:9); God the Son (Gen. 18:1ff., God in bodily form; John 8:36); God the Holy Spirit (Gen 1:2; John 14:26).

This truth came through divine revelation and not through human reason. Endeavoring to express the many elements of God's nature, man made many gods. But God revealed Himself as one God who bears several relationships to man. The triune God is clearly seen at Jesus' baptism (Matt. 3:13–17). Furthermore, in all three manifestations He is seen as active in both creation and redemption.

God the Father

The fatherhood of God in the Christian sense, though implied, is not taught distinctly in the Old Testament. However, in both Testaments God is seen as reigning in providential care over His creation and His creatures. He directs the flow of human history according to His redemptive purpose. This is evidenced in God's choice of Abraham and his descendants, the nation of Israel, and that nation's relationships to other nations. Thus one sees within history God's holy history, wherein He directs the affairs of men and nations toward the fulfillment of His redemptive purpose. As Father, God is infinite in love, power, and wisdom. As Father, God cares for all of His creation.

The clear revelation of God as Father came through Jesus. Jesus called God His Father, and to His disciples He spoke of God as their Father. This distinction is clearly seen in John 20:17. "I ascend unto my Father, and your Father; and to my God, and your God."

Jesus is God's Son essentially and eternally. Men may become sons of God through faith in Jesus Christ. The universal fatherhood of God is a beautiful ideal, but is not a reality. All men are God's creatures, but as such are not God's children. God is fatherly in His attitude toward all men. He wills that all men shall be His children. But He is Father in truth only to those who become His children through faith in His Son.

God the Son

Christ is the eternal Son of God. He is the key to man's knowledge of God and history. The Old Testament sounds the messianic hope. The Gospels record Christ's incarnation; Acts relates His continuing work through the Holy Spirit; the Epistles interpret His person and work; Revelation proclaims His final triumph and glory. As individuals read the Bible, it is essential that they keep in mind that Christ is central.

His names.—There are no fewer than 80 names given in the Bible to declare Christ's person, nature, and work. Certain of these may be noted briefly.

Christ is His official title. It is the Greek equivalent of the Hebrew *Messiah, the anointed for salvation.* Since to His Jewish contemporaries it carried political and military connotations, He never used it in personal reference except in a private conversation (John 4:25–26). With His approval, He allowed His disciples to use it in private (Matt. 16:17). But He forbade them to proclaim Him as such until after His ascension (v. 20). Only then would they understand the spiritual nature of the term. To avoid perjury under oath He admitted that He was the Christ (Matt. 26:63–64). This official title came to be used as a personal name.

Jesus is the human, saving name of the Son. It is the Greek equivalent of the Hebrew *Joshua* meaning *Jehovah is salvation* (Matt. 1:21; Acts 4:12).

Lord is another name of the Son. In the New Testament, when used of Jesus in the purely Christian sense, it means *Jehovah in the flesh* (1 Pet. 3:15). Thomas declared Jesus to be "my Lord and my God" (John 20:28).

Word, as referring to Christ, is found only in John's writings. It means an open, spoken manifestation. *Logos* was used by Greek philosophers to refer to the principle which controls the universe or the soul of the world. But John's usage seems to be purely Hebrew in nature, though it also may have been colored by the philosophical use.

John introduced the "Word" with the phrase "in the beginning" (John 1:1), suggesting a relationship to Genesis 1:1. Each phase of God's creative work was introduced by "and God said"; hence a *logos*, an open, spoken manifestation of God in His creative work. John used "Word" to indicate that Christ was also God's open, spoken manifestation in redemption.

Son of Man was Jesus' favorite self-designation, stressing His humanity. Messianic in nature, it carried no political-military sense. It suggests Christ's identity with man for his redemption. In the Gospels it was used only by Jesus except when quoted by His questioners. After Acts 7:56 it does not appear again until Revelation 1:13, where Christ is seen as indwelling His churches.

Son of God was used by both Jesus and others to stress His deity. However, only demons used this title in direct address to Jesus. But under oath He admitted that He was the Son of God (Matt. 26:63–64).

Some critics deny that Jesus ever claimed deity for Himself. However, His abundant use of "Son" in relation to God as Father negates such a denial. Note John 10:30: "I and my Father are one." The Jewish leaders saw this as a direct claim to deity. They proposed to stone Him for blasphemy "because that thou, being a man, makest thyself God" (John 10:33).

His deity-humanity.—"In the beginning was the Word, and the Word was with [face to face with, equal to] God, and the Word was God" (John 1:1). Thus John declared Christ to be coeternal, coequal, and coexistent with God. The four uses of "was" in verses 1–2 render a form of the verb meaning "always was." There never was a time when this was not true.

As deity, Christ was active in the creation of the universe (John 1:3). Literally, "Every single part of the universe came into being through him; and apart from him not even one thing came into being which was come into being." Paul expressed the same thought, only he saw the universe as a whole (Col. 1:16–17). Literally, "In the sphere of him was created the universe as a whole... the universe as a whole through him and unto him stands created. And he and he alone is before any single part of the universe, and the universe as a whole in him holds together." He created the universe. The more man learns about the universe, the greater is his concept of Christ.

Perhaps the greatest single verse on the deity of Christ is Colossians 2:9. Literally, "For in him and him alone is permanently at home every single part of the very essence of deity, the state of being God in bodily form." He is the source of life, both the animal principle of life and spiritual life.

And yet He who always was coeternal, coequal, and coexistent with God "was made flesh, and dwelt among us ... full of grace and truth" (John 1:14). He who always was God Himself became a flesh-and-blood man that He might redeem men from sin.

It is true that Jesus Christ was God. But even more wonderful, God became Jesus of Nazareth! He is the very essence of grace and truth. When God would reveal His law, He did so through a man, Moses. But when He revealed His grace, He became a man, Jesus Christ. And He did so through a birth that is unique in history.

His virgin birth.—That Jesus was born of a virgin is clearly stated in the Scriptures. Some question this on two grounds: that it is recorded only by Matthew and Luke; and that it is contrary to the natural laws of genetics.

As for the former, how many times must an event be recorded in the Bible to be true? Mark's Gospel begins with Jesus' public ministry, thus would pass over His birth and childhood. John does not record it since it had been told in previous Gospels. However, he implies it in 1:14. How else could God become a flesh-and-blood man? Paul, while not affirming the virgin birth, certainly implies it in Galatians 4:4. No question was raised in Christian history about Jesus' virgin birth, except by His enemies (John 8:41), until the eighteenth or nineteenth century. Had it been untrue when the Gospels were written, there were many people alive, perhaps Mary herself, who could have refuted the story.

The virgin birth is fully recorded in two of the Gospels. Matthew records it when he says that Jesus was conceived of the Holy Spirit, and is careful to show that Joseph was not Jesus' father (1:18–20).

Luke was a physician whose medical language rates him along with Galen and Hippocrates. As a scientist, he knew how to ferret out facts and evaluate evidence. It is even possible that he may have talked with Mary herself, who would reveal intimate details of Jesus' birth to a physician. All of Luke's training would militate against the idea of a virgin birth. Yet the evidence was so conclusive that he records the most complete account of Jesus' birth on record (1:26–38; 2:1–19). Despite careful critical scrutiny, not one demonstrable historical error has been proved against him. Consistency in unbiased research compels one to accept his account at face value.[3]

But what about the laws of genetics? It should be noted that Mary herself raised the first question about the virgin birth (Luke 1:34). Note the angel's answer. "For with God nothing shall be impossible" (v. 37). What God says, He can do.

Is the virgin birth impossible? Even man can cause birth through artificial insemination. This should not be confused with Jesus' birth. But if man can do that, who is to say what God can or cannot do? One must not limit God's power by man's power. Laws of genetics unknown to man are known to God.

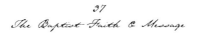

The Son of God could be born by no other type of birth than that stated in the Gospels. To people of faith, no word is needed except Luke 1:35. "The Holy Ghost shall come upon thee, and the power of the Highest shall overshadow thee: therefore also that holy thing which shall be born of thee shall be called the Son of God."

His sinless life.—Cynics may question the manner of Jesus' birth, but not His character. He perfectly revealed God as holiness, righteousness, truth, and love. He did the will of His Father always. "For he hath made him to be sin for us, who knew no sin" (2 Cor. 5:21).

Jesus lived in a flesh and blood body in a corrupt world. He completely identified himself with man apart from sin. In all points he was tempted like as men are, yet without sin. But not one error or sin of His is to be found in the trophy hall of Satan. Even His enemies could find no fault in Him.

Someone pointed out that Jesus' perfect life in a corrupt world was as great a miracle in the moral sphere as was his virgin birth in the physical sphere. Because of His perfect life, Jesus is qualified to save men from their sins (Heb. 5:8–9).

His atoning death.—Paul described Jesus as one "whom God hath set forth to be a propitiation [grounds for forgiveness] through faith in his blood, to declare his righteousness for the remission of sins that are past, through the forbearance of God; to declare ... at this time his righteousness: that he might be just, and the justifier of him which believeth in Jesus" (Rom. 3:25–26).

Note the words "just" and "justifier." In his perfect life Jesus justified God in His demand for righteousness in man. He demonstrated that one can live in a flesh and blood body in a corrupt world, be tempted in all points, yet not sin. Having proved God just, in His death on the cross He paid the price for sin and thus became the justifier before God of all who believe in Him as Savior.

Jesus' death was vicarious in nature. He died for the sins of people. Said he, "I am the good shepherd: the good shepherd giveth his life for his sheep" (John 10:11). It pictures one throwing his body over another to take his punishment in himself. Jesus did this for lost people. On the cross, therefore, he endured in himself the whole of God's wrath against sin. His death was voluntary. No man took his life; he gave it freely. And it was a once-for-all death. There will be no other Savior; no other is needed. "But now once [once for all] in the end of the world [age] hath he appeared to put away sin by the sacrifice of himself. ... So Christ was once [once for all] offered to bear the sins of many" (Heb. 9:26–28).

His triumphant resurrection.—Had Jesus died and done nothing more, he would have been a martyr but not a Savior. The glorious truth is that "Christ died for our sins according to the scriptures ... and that he rose again the third day according to the scriptures" (1 Cor. 15:3–4). Thus He is the Son of God with power to save by His resurrection from the dead. He is both the crucified Savior and the living Lord.

The bodily resurrection of Jesus is one of the best authenticated events in all of history. All four Gospels acclaim it, and the remainder of the New Testament proclaims it.

As with Jesus' birth, Luke, the physician-scientist-historian, gives the most complete account of it. All efforts to deny or explain the empty tomb away have failed.[4]

The resurrection proves the deity of Christ. It makes effective His death. It assures believers of Jesus' daily companionship. And it is the guarantee of the Christian's own bodily resurrection.

His mediatorial reign.—Forty days after His resurrection, Jesus ascended to the right hand of the Father (Acts 1:9). There He is reigning in His mediatorial kingdom (1 Cor. 15:25). And He looks to that time when He shall present a redeemed natural and spiritual universe unto the Father, that God (Father, Son, Holy Spirit) may be all in all (1 Cor. 15:24–28). At the end of the age He will return in great glory and power.

In the meantime, he is the one Mediator whereby lost persons may be reconciled to God (2 Cor. 5:19–21). A mediator is one appointed to bring together two estranged parties. He must perfectly represent both parties and do all that is necessary to bring them together. As the God-man, Jesus does this. He partakes of the nature of both God and man, and in Him they meet in reconciliation.

Jesus is still God and man. And he indwells all believers as the living and ever-present Lord.

God the Holy Spirit

The Holy Spirit is the "Spirit of God" and the "Spirit of Christ." Thus He is God in spiritual manifestation. As God is a person, so is the Holy Spirit a Person. He possesses all the attributes of God, and all elements of personality.

The meaning of the name.—The Hebrew word for spirit meant, originally, *breath*; later, *wind*; and finally, *Spirit*. The Greek equivalent connotes an intangible substance which possesses great power for constructive or destructive use according to one's relationship to it. In the Bible, *Spirit* is always associated with power or force. As the word *Spirit* came to be used of God, it took the quality of holiness, hence, Holy Spirit. Unfortunately, the *King James Version* renders "Spirit" as "Ghost."

The Holy Spirit in the Scriptures.—The Holy Spirit is presented in both the Old and New Testaments. But as with other revelations of God, He is presented more clearly in the New Testament.

In the Old Testament the Holy Spirit is seen as active in creation. He came upon men to enable them to do mighty works for God. Wisdom and skill came from the Holy Spirit, who endowed the prophets with wisdom and revealed God's truth to them. He was present in men in ethical power and was the anointing power for the Messiah.

In the New Testament He was the agent in Jesus' conception (Matt. 1:18). He was present at Jesus' baptism and temptations. Jesus worked in the power of the Holy Spirit. Note that He performed no miracles that are recorded in the Bible until after His anointing by the Spirit at His baptism.

Jesus sent forth His disciples in the power of the Holy Spirit (Matt. 10:16–20). He went to the cross in the "eternal Spirit" (Heb. 9:14). He was raised from the dead according to the Spirit of holiness (Rom. 1:4). Before His death Jesus promised the coming of the Holy Spirit in power (Luke 24:49; John 14:16–18; Acts 1:8), a promise which was fulfilled at Pentecost (Acts 2). Acts records the Holy Spirit's work through believers to carry on the work which Jesus began. The remainder of the New Testament does likewise, as the writers interpreted the meaning of the person and work of Jesus Christ.

Work of the Holy Spirit.—The Holy Spirit is the Spirit of God sent forth to do His work. General mention of this has been made in preceding paragraphs. There are four specific works worthy of further details.

The first is related to the Scriptures themselves. This has to do with revelation, inspiration, and illumination (see chapter 2). The Holy Spirit revealed God's will. He inspired chosen ones to record it. And He illumines minds so that they may understand it.

The second work of the Holy Spirit is related to administration. His work through men, even through Jesus, was in this regard. It is seen most clearly in the Book of Acts. At Pentecost He transformed the disciples from defeatism to boldness, giving them a full understanding of Jesus' redemptive work. He enabled them to speak in languages other than their native tongues, thus enabling them to preach to the people gathered in Jerusalem. He stood with them before their opponents. He guided early Christians in their decisions. Each new development in the preaching of the gospel was at the expressed command or with the approval of the Holy Spirit.

The third work of the Spirit is with lost people. Jesus said that the Holy Spirit convicts of sin, righteousness, and judgment (John 16:8–11). He convicts men of their sin, showing that the greatest sin is lack of faith in Jesus Christ; of righteousness which God demands, which they lack, and which they can have only in Christ; and of judgment under which they abide as children of Satan. Thus one recognizes God's just judgment, and is ready to receive Christ unto salvation or to reject Him unto condemnation.

The Holy Spirit enables a lost sinner to turn to Christ in faith. And in His power to be born of the Holy Spirit as a child of God. He seals and sanctifies such as God's possession.

The fourth specific work of the Holy Spirit is with the Christian. When one becomes a Christian, the Holy Spirit takes up His abode in that person's life. Thus Paul speaks of the Christian as the temple of the Holy Spirit. Through Christians, He also dwells in the churches.

Before Jesus returned to the Father, He promised that the Holy Spirit would come to be with His followers. "And I will pray the Father, and he shall give you another comforter, that he may abide with you forever" (John 14:16). "Another" means another of the same kind, like Jesus. The Holy Spirit comforts in sorrow, encourages in depression, and exhorts to high endeavor and holy living for Christ. He teaches, guides, and brings understanding of God's revealed and recorded word. What He hears from the Father He speaks. He endows Christians with spiritual gifts with which to serve God.

The Holy Spirit does not reveal Himself; He reveals God in Christ, which is one explanation as to why one understands Jesus better than the Spirit. Jesus said, "He shall glorify me: for he shall receive of mine, and shall shew it unto you" (John 16:14). He shall glorify Me! Not Himself. Which suggests that any system of religion or theology which magnifies the Holy Spirit above Jesus is not of the Holy Spirit!

One final thought calls for consideration—that of being filled with the Holy Spirit. Paul said, "And be not drunk with wine ... but be filled with the Spirit" (Eph. 5:18). Used in this connection, the point seems to be that one should get buoyancy and exhilaration—not for a limited time through alcohol—and should have a permanent lift and glow through surrender to the Holy Spirit in one's life.

Jesus taught that the Holy Spirit indwells every Christian (John 14:16–17). One may be filled with the Holy Spirit but not filled with His power. To be filled with the Holy Spirit, one must be submissive and available to the indwelling Spirit. It is not how much of the Holy Spirit the Christian has, but how much of the Christian the Holy Spirit has.

The New Testament does not teach a second blessing or second baptism of the Holy Spirit. In Acts, other than with regard to the assembled church, the Holy Spirit came upon individuals only in connection with their regenerating experience. In Ephesus, Paul questioned John the Baptist's disciples (Acts 19:2). This verse reads like a "second blessing." But a literal rendering is "Did you receive the Holy Spirit when you believed?" When they did believe in Jesus, the Holy Spirit came upon them. So the presence of the Holy Spirit in one's life is evidence of regeneration, not of a "second blessing" or of sanctification as some regard it (see chapter 5).

Of interest is the fact that "the fruit of the Spirit" is not some ecstatic manifestation. It is "love, joy, peace, longsuffering, gentleness, goodness, faith, meekness, temperance" (Gal. 5:22–23).

To live in the Spirit, one should walk in the Spirit and thus glorify God—Father, Son, and Holy Spirit. "For the fruit of the Spirit is in all goodness and righteousness and truth" (Eph. 5:9).

SOME QUESTIONS FOR FURTHER THOUGHT

1. How can God be three in one? Can you think of ways in which you are one person, yet bear three relationships to other people?

2. What is the difference between Jesus as the Son of God and Christians as sons of God? How can Jesus be both God and man? Is belief in Jesus' virgin birth and resurrection vital to Christian faith? Does the fact that you cannot explain them by natural law as you understand it mean that they are not true?

four
MAN

Man was created by the special act of God, in His own image, and is the crowning work of His creation. In the beginning man was innocent of sin and was endowed by his creator with freedom of choice. By his free choice man sinned against God and brought sin into the human race. Through the temptation of Satan man transgressed the command of God, and fell from his original innocence; whereby his posterity inherit a nature and an environment inclined toward sin, and as soon as they are capable of moral action become transgressors and are under condemnation. Only the grace of God can bring man into His holy fellowship and enable man to fulfill the creative purpose of God. The sacredness of human personality is evident in that God created man in His own image, and in that Christ died for man; therefore every man possesses dignity and is worthy of respect and Christian love.

Gen. 1:26–30; 2:5,7,18–22; 3; 9:6; Ps. 1; 8:3–6; 32:1–5; 51:5; Isa. 6:5; Jer. 17:5; Matt. 16:26; Acts 17:26–31; Rom. 1:19–32; 3:10–18,23; 5:6,12,19; 6:6; 7:14–25; 8:14–18,29; 1 Cor. 1:21–31; 15:19,21–22; Eph. 2:1–22; Col. 1:21–22; 3:9–11

"Man was created by the special act of God, in His own image, and is the crowning work of His creation." The creation of man is simply stated in the Bible. "So God created man in his own image. ... And the Lord God formed man of the dust of the ground, and breathed into his nostrils the breath of life; and man became a living soul" (Gen 1:27; 2:7). It should be noted that this came as the climax of God's creative work. It was not an afterthought with God, but the goal of his work in creation.

Three things may be noted about man. His body is akin to the natural elements. His physical life is akin to all animal life. But as a living soul he is made in God's image and likeness. It should be noted that man was made to live forever. It was after he had sinned that he became subject to death. However, for that reason man's animal principle of life shall cease; his body shall return to the ground (see Gen. 3:19). But his soul, the real person, is immortal. It will never cease to be.

Man is twofold in nature. He is both spirit and body. Man is not a body and has a soul. He is a soul and has a body. The body is mortal; the soul is immortal.

Only of man is it said that he was made in God's image. Since God is Spirit, this image relates to man's spiritual nature. This divine image means that

The Baptist Faith & Message

God created man with a rational, emotional, and moral nature. He possesses a will with the freedom of choice. In his original creation, man was in a state of innocence with the possibility that he might choose righteousness or sinfulness. God's image in man is also seen in that he was to have dominion over the lower orders of creation.

Personal Learning Activity 5

Draw a picture (image, symbol) to depict man as body, soul, and spirit. Write a paragraph to explain your drawing.

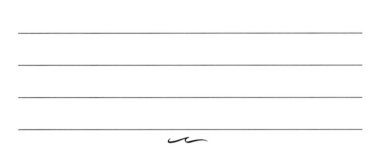

_____

_____

_____

_____

Psalm 8:5 reads, "For thou hast made him a little lower than the angels, and hast crowned him with glory and honour." However, the Hebrew text reads, "For thou has made him a little lower than God *[Elohim]*." Thus man was created more than an angel. He was a little lower than God!

The Fall of Man

Created in a state of innocence, man was neither righteous nor sinful. Before becoming either he must exercise the right of choice, hence the temptation experience in the garden of Eden. So God permitted man to be tempted or tested by the serpent (Gen. 3). The Bible does not deal with the origin of evil. It assumes it, relates its destructive power, and shows how God deals with the problem.

In Eden, God made provision for every need of man. "And the Lord God commanded the man, saying, Of every tree of the garden thou mayest freely eat: but of the tree of the knowledge of good and evil, thou shalt not eat of it: for in the day that thou eatest thereof thou shalt surely die" (Gen 2:16–17). It is idle speculation to try to determine what kind of tree this was. Perhaps its fruit may be regarded as symbolizing the determination to build a social order outside the will of God. To say the least, this was the result of man's decision to eat the fruit contrary to God's will. And this willful decision constituted sin.

In the Bible sin is described as crookedness, violence, lawlessness, iniquity, wickedness, offense, and rebellion. Sin may be defined as rebellion against God's will. The root of sin is selfishness, centering one's life about oneself rather than in God. God does not classify sins as large or small, heavy or light. Any transgression of God's will is sin (Jas. 2:9–11). The greatest sin is unbelief with respect to Jesus Christ (John 3:18).

The account of man's fall is found in Genesis 3:1–7. "Now the serpent was more subtil than any beast of the field" (v. 1). Note that Satan disguised himself. In the Bible he always appears before God in his true light (Job 1–2; Matt. 4). But he never appears to man as such. He probably appeared to Eve as a beautiful, graceful creature, not as a snake crawling on the ground (Gen. 3:14).

Approaching Eve, the serpent questioned God's goodness and love (v. 1). He did not point to God's bountiful provision but to his one prohibition, failing to note that it was for man's good. In her innocence the woman showed her tendency toward righteousness by protesting on behalf of God's purpose (vv. 2–3). Satan countered by calling God a liar. "Ye shall not surely die" (v. 4). He said that God was holding out on man, thus depriving him of his full potential. "For God doth know that in the day ye eat thereof, then your eyes shall be opened, and ye shall be as gods, knowing good and evil" (v. 5).

In this verse one sees the very nature of sin. For "gods" renders *Elohim*, God. So, "ye shall be as God." Man was made a little lower than God (Ps. 8:5). It is when man through selfish ambition seeks to be God in his own life and will that he sins. Sin is dethroning God and enthroning self. It was this very thing which snared Eve, which shows that she also had a tendency toward sin. And this tendency overcame her tendency toward righteousness.

"And when the woman saw that the tree was good for food, and that it was pleasant to the eyes, and a tree to be desired to make one wise, she took of the fruit thereof, and did eat, and gave also unto her husband with her; and he did eat" (v. 6).

Several years ago a resolution was presented at the SBC regarding a woman's place in God's service. One "whereas" was to the effect that it was through woman that sin entered the human race. But read Genesis 3:1–6. Eve heard from Adam of God's mandate about the forbidden fruit; Adam heard it directly from God. It required all of Satan's wiles to catch Eve. What led Adam to eat the fruit? *Eve offered it to him.* Traditionally woman has been the *conscience* of the race. Paul said that it was in Adam, not Eve, that all die or are separated from God (1 Cor. 15:22).

Here are the three general areas of temptation: physical appetite ("good for food"); aesthetic nature ("pleasant to the eyes"); ambition ("desired to make

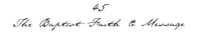

one wise"). These are the three areas in which the devil tempted Jesus: physical appetite (turn stones to bread, Matt. 4:3); aesthetic nature (jump from the Temple, Matt. 4:6); ambition (receive worldly kingdoms by worshiping Satan, Matt. 4:9). Luke 4:13 calls these "all the temptation," or every kind of temptation. Satan failed to snare Jesus, but succeeded with Eve and Adam (Gen. 3:7). W. Kersey Davis discussed sin as an illegitimate expression of a legitimate desire.

Satan does not tempt man in his lower but in his higher nature. He seeks to get him to express his God-given powers in a lower manner (Jas. 1:14–15). Commenting along this same line Conner says: "So the devil tempted Eve by appealing to these three desires that are normal in any healthy human being. Wherein, then consisted her sin? In trying to satisfy these normal desires of her being in the wrong way, contrary to the will of God. ...Sin is the perversion of the good and the worst sin may be the perversion of the best. ... Not the use but the abuse of God's world causes trouble. ... Sin always appears in the guise of a good. Otherwise it would be no temptation."[1]

When man sinned he was separated from God. The fellowship was broken; the image was destroyed. Adam and Eve died physically many years later. However, the moment that they chose Satan's will instead of God's will, they died spiritually. They were no longer innocent. Certainly they were not righteous. They were sinners lost from God.

They were driven from God's presence, for a holy God cannot condone sin. Their sin had separated them and their God. Furthermore, their bodies became subject to the ills and pains of life. It should be noted that while God hates sin, he loves the sinner. Even in Eden, before he pronounced judgment upon man, he threw out the promise of redemption (Gen. 3:15). Therefore, this verse is called the gospel before the gospel; it foreshadows the Redeemer.

The story of Adam and Eve is the history of the human race, because all their posterity inherit the same tendency toward sin. "And as soon as they are capable of moral action become transgressors and are under condemnation."

Dignity of Human Personality

Despite the fact of man's sordid record, he still remains the crown of God's creation. Even as a sinner he is the object of God's eternal love as seen in the fact that Christ died to save him (Rom. 5:8). It follows naturally, therefore, that man is of infinite worth in God's sight. "God is no respecter of persons" (Acts 10:34). For this reason "every man possesses dignity and is worthy of respect and Christian love."

SOME QUESTIONS FOR FURTHER THOUGHT

1. Make a comparative study of the temptations of Eve and Jesus. Note especially the three areas of temptation in Genesis 3:6 and Matthew 4:1–11. Recall your own experiences in temptation. How may you learn from Jesus' experience ways to resist temptation?

2. What is your attitude toward other people created in God's image?

SALVATION

Salvation involves the redemption of the whole man, and is offered freely to all who accept Jesus Christ as Lord and Savior, who by His own blood obtained eternal redemption for the believer. In its broadest sense salvation includes regeneration, sanctification, and glorification.

A. Regeneration, or the new birth, is a work of God's grace whereby believers become new creatures in Christ Jesus. It is a change of heart wrought by the Holy Spirit through conviction of sin, to which the sinner responds in repentance toward God and faith in the Lord Jesus Christ.

Repentance and faith are inseparable experiences of grace. Repentance is a genuine turning from sin toward God. Faith is the acceptance of Jesus Christ and commitment of the entire personality to Him as Lord and Savior. Justification is God's gracious and full acquittal upon principles of His righteousness of all sinners who repent and believe in Christ. Justification brings the believer into a relationship of peace and favor with God.

B. Sanctification is the experience, beginning in regeneration, by which the believer is set apart to God's purposes, and is enabled to progress toward moral and spiritual perfection through the presence and power of the Holy Spirit dwelling in him. Growth in grace should continue throughout the regenerate person's life.

C. Glorification is the culmination of salvation and is the final blessed and abiding state of the redeemed.

Gen 3:15; Ex. 3:14–17; 6:2–8; Matt. 1:21; 4:17; 16:21–26; 27:22 to 28:6; Luke 1:68–69; 2:28–32; John 1:11–14,29; 3:3–21,36; 5:24; 10:9,28–29; 15:1–16; 17:17; Acts 2:21; 4:12; 15:11; 16:30–31; 17:30–31; 20:32; Rom. 1:16–18; 2:4; 3:23–25; 4:3 ff.; 5:8–10; 6:1–23; 8:1–18,29–39; 10:9–10,13; 13:11–14; 1 Cor. 1:18,30; 6:19–20; 15:10; 2 Cor. 5:17–20; Gal. 2:20; 3:13; 5:22–25; 6:15; Eph. 1:7; 2:8–22; 4:11–16; Phil. 2:12–13; Col. 1:9–22; 3:1 ff.; 1 Thess. 5:23–24; 2 Tim. 1:12; Titus 2:11–14; Heb. 2:1–3; 5:8–9; 9:24–28; 11:1 to 12:8,14; James 2:14–26; 1 Pet. 1:2–23; 1 John 1:6 to 2:11; Rev. 3:20; 21:1 to 22:5

The word salvation has various meanings in the Scriptures. For instance, in the New Testament this word and its verb form are sometimes used in the sense of rescuing from danger or destruction (Matt. 8:25; Acts 27:20) and of healing from disease (Matt. 9:22), or even solving a problem (Phil. 2:12). But its greatest use is with regard to spiritual salvation through Christ (Matt. 19:25; John 3:17).

Salvation in this sense means the full redemption of whole man. To redeem is to buy back something. God paid the ransom to himself in order to satisfy the demands of his holy, righteous nature. This he did through Jesus' death and resurrection. "God was in Christ, reconciling the world unto himself" (2 Cor. 5:19). On the cross Jesus Christ made the once-for-all sacrifice for the sins of men. "Neither by the blood of goats and calves, but by his own blood he entered in once into the holy place, having obtained eternal redemption for us" (Heb. 9:12).

This salvation was and is offered to believers on God's initiative as an expression of his love for sinners. "For God so loved the world, that he gave his only begotten Son, that whosoever believeth in him should not perish, but have everlasting life" (John 3:16). This everlasting or eternal life is not a life that begins after death. It is that quality of life which is eternal, beginning the moment one believes in Jesus and continuing in eternity.

Way of Salvation

Sin separated man from God. The fellowship depicted in Eden was broken. But God proposed to restore it. At Sinai he gave his law to Israel (Ex. 20). In essence, Paul says that God wrote this same law into the hearts of pagans (Rom. 2:14–16). In a sense God called from the heights of his holiness for man to come up to him. Failure to do so brought judgment in keeping with either code of law given to man (Rom. 2:1–13). Jesus himself told the rich young ruler that to inherit eternal life he must keep the commandments (Matt. 19:16–17). But they must be kept perfectly. Failure in one law made one as guilty as though he had failed in all. No man does as good as he knows. So no man keeps God's law perfectly, whether it be the written law or that in pagan hearts. Someone may object that God is unjust in making such a demand. The perfect life of Jesus speaks to the contrary. He proved God "just" in his demand for perfect righteousness. Having done so, God in Christ became the "justifier of him which believeth in Jesus" (Rom. 3:26). This he did by paying the price for each person's sin in his atoning death, that through faith in him we might receive the righteousness of God which is in his Son.

Personal Learning Activity 6

Read the following Scripture references and write a definition of sin using each reference: Genesis 6:5; Jeremiah 17:9; Galatians 5:19–21; John 16:8–9; Romans 3:10–23; James 4:17; Psalm 51:4.

Genesis 6:5: _____

The Baptist Faith & Message

Jeremiah 17:9: _____

Galatians 5:19–21: _____

John 16:8–9: _____

Romans 3:10–23: _____

James 4:17: _____

Psalm 51:4: _____

What sins cause you the greatest concern? Why? _____

_____

_____

⤳⤳

This is the sense of Galatians 4:4–5. Jesus was "made under the law, to redeem them that were under the law, that we might receive the adoption of sons." Jesus came to seek and to save that which was lost. And this salvation is offered freely to all who receive Jesus Christ as Lord and Savior.

This means that salvation is by grace through faith in Jesus Christ. When man would not, could not be saved by the law, God provided salvation by grace through faith. By his sordid, sinful record, man proved that he would not obey God's law.

If God knew from the beginning that this would be true, why did he wait so long to provide salvation through His Son? God knew it. But man had to learn by bitter experience that he was too weak and willful to be saved by law. This knowledge of man is involved in "the fulness of the time" (Gal 4:4). It was a time right in God's wisdom. When man would not, could not save himself, he was ready for someone else to do it for him. So in Christ God did for man what neither he, no one else, nor anything else could do for him. That is the very essence of grace. C. Roy Angell once said that grace means that God gives us what we need, not what we deserve.

Originally the Greek word rendered "grace" meant to make a gift, then to forgive a debt, then to forgive a wrong, and finally to forgive sin. So basically grace is a gift, as expressed in Romans 3:24. Literally, "Being declared righteous as a gift by his grace through the full redemption, the one in Christ Jesus."

This truth is plainly stated in Ephesians 2:8–10. "For by grace are ye saved through faith; and that not of [out of] yourselves: it is the gift of God: not of [out of] works, lest any man should boast. For we are his workmanship, created in Christ Jesus unto good works, which God hath before ordained that we should walk in them."

Note that salvation is not "out of yourselves" or "out of works" as the source. It is "of God the gift." It is by grace made possible in the individual through his faith. Good works are the fruit, not the root, of salvation.

In the first century the Jews regarded themselves as God's children. They performed righteous deeds in order to be rewarded by God. Paul notes that by such deeds of self-righteousness they failed to receive the righteousness of God (Rom. 10—11). Thinking that salvation was for Jews only, certain Jewish Christians (Judaizers) preached that Gentiles must first become Jewish proselytes, then believe in Jesus, in order to be saved (Acts 15:1). But Peter said, "But we believe that through the grace of the Lord Jesus Christ we [Jews] shall be saved, even as they [Gentiles]" (Acts 15:11). Rather than for Gentiles to be saved as Jews, Jews must be saved the same as Gentiles, by grace through faith.

This same truth is expressed in the word "righteousness" as used in Romans 1:17. The Greek word so translated belongs to a family of words which means that a thing is not necessarily true, but which one chooses to regard as being true. In discussing God's righteousness (chapter 3), three uses of the word were noted: what God is in His nature, what He demands in man, and what He bestows in Christ. In Romans 1:16, the third sense is stated. You may wish to review these concepts in chapter 3.

Thus here the "righteousness of God" is not an attribute of God, but an activity of God. By it God picks one up out of the wrong and puts him down in the right as though he had never been in the wrong. It does not mean that one is righteous within himself, but that one in Christ is so regarded. He has the righteousness of God which is in Christ Jesus (Rom. 10:1–10). And note that it is a matter of faith from beginning to end. It is by grace through faith.

Salvation in the larger sense may be seen as threefold: regeneration, sanctification, glorification. The context in each case must decide its meaning. Failure to recognize this distinction leads to many errors, such as believing in salvation by works, believing in falling from grace, and uncertainty as to one's salvation until one appears before the judgment seat of Christ (Heb. 9:28). But when this distinction is preserved, it adds to the meaning of the experience of salvation in its larger sense.

Regeneration

Regeneration is the experience of being born again or from above (John 3:3; Titus 3:5). It is an instantaneous work of God's grace wrought by the Holy Spirit through faith in Jesus Christ. Thus the believer becomes a new creation in Christ Jesus (2 Cor. 5:16). Note that to create is a work of God, not of man

(Eph. 2:10). The second one is born again, he is a child of God, a finished relationship which cannot be broken.

While Jesus used the vital figure of life, Paul expressed the same thought in the legal term "adoption" (Rom. 8:15; Gal 4:5; Eph. 1:5). Literally, "the placing in the position of a son." Under Roman law one person, usually a slave, might be adopted into the family of another. A price was paid by the adopting father in the presence of witnesses. He assumed all the obligations of the new son. The son was considered as being born again into a new family. He received the privileges of sonship, including heirship, along with naturally born sons. He also assumed the responsibilities of sonship (Rom. 8:17).

Regeneration is the result of conviction of sin, repentance from sin, faith in Jesus Christ, and the confession of that faith. Conviction is the state of mind and heart whereby lost persons recognize and admit their sinful states and practices. It is a work wrought by the Holy Spirit (John 16:8). Under conviction one will either reject Christ and plunge deeper into sin or else receive Christ as Savior. But conviction itself is not regeneration.

Conviction must be followed by true repentance. Two Greek verbs are translated repent. One means to regret something, or to feel remorse, but does not imply a change of one's nature (Matt. 27:3). The other means a change of mind, heart, and attitude. It involves a change of attitude—from hating God to loving him; from loving sin to hating it. Thus one abhors sin not only because of what it does to one's self but to God. This is true repentance necessary for regeneration.

True repentance will be followed by faith. Indeed, repentance and faith are inseparable experiences of grace. Truly repentant persons will turn to Jesus Christ in faith as Savior. Faith means to believe. But in its truest sense it is more than intellectual. It involves an act of the will whereby one trusts in Christ and commits one's self to him, to his will and way. It means to accept or receive Christ as both Lord and Savior. Thus one will be brought to confess him as such (Rom. 10: 9–10).

It is thus that one is regenerated, declared righteous as justified before God. But it is not the end of the Christian experience. It is the beginning. Someone asked Gaines S. Dobbins if conversion was not the end of evangelism. He replied, "Yes, but which end?"

Sanctification

Unfortunately, because some groups have related the idea of sanctification with the "second blessing" and sinless perfection, many Baptists seem to be afraid of the word. It has been noted previously that the Bible does not teach a "second blessing." Neither does it teach sinless perfection as a reality in the Christian's life. First John was written to Christian people (1 John 1:8 to 2:1).

Sanctification is related to holy. It means the state of being set apart or dedicated to the services of God. Thus Christians are called saints, or dedicated, holy, sanctified ones (1 Cor. 1:2; 2 Cor. 1:1). Corinthian Christians did not always act saintly. But they were saints nevertheless.

The burden of Scripture is to the effect that sanctification is an instantaneous experience whereby the regenerated one is set apart to God's service. Thereafter, he should grow, develop, and serve in the state of sanctification (Heb 2:3). This idea is inherent in both the new birth and adoption.

In this sense, therefore, Christian people are called "a holy nation." As Israel in the Old Testament was set apart for God's service, so in the New Testament this people is identified with the followers of Christ. Of interest is the fact that whereas in the Old Testament holy is primarily related to things, in the New Testament sense it relates principally to people.

Sanctification is a work of the Holy Spirit (Rom. 15:16). He indwells the Christian and seeks to develop and use him in God's service. That sanctify does not refer basically to a riddance of sin is clear from John 17:19 where Jesus said, "I sanctify myself." He dedicated himself to God's redemptive purpose by way of the cross. But he also prayed that his followers "also might be sanctified through the truth" (v. 19). In the truth of the gospel they were/are sanctified or set apart for God's service. But as sanctified vessels they should seek to abstain from evil. The Christian life is the sanctified life. As such it should seek progressively to be rid of sin and more suited to God's use.

The glory of the gospel is that souls are regenerated. But the tragedy is that so many Christian lives are lost to God's service through an incomplete understanding of sanctification. All should heed the words of Peter, literally, "But go on growing in grace and in the knowledge of our Lord and Saviour Jesus Christ" (2 Pet. 3:18).

Glorification

"Glorification is the culmination of salvation and is the final blessed and abiding state of the redeemed." It is the ultimate and complete salvation which shall be realized in heaven (Rom. 8:29–30; Heb. 9:28).

In Ephesians 1:14 Paul speaks of "the redemption of the purchased possession." "Redemption" should read "full redemption." It sums up the total salvation with emphasis upon glorification. For that which God has purchased in Christ he will keep in him. And he will glorify it in heaven, meaning the final resurrection of the body (Rom. 8:23, "redemption" here the same as in Eph. 1:14) and the sum-total of glory and reward in heaven.

It should be noted that the Christian is heir to the privileges of sonship but also to the sufferings of the same (Rom. 8:17). He is to suffer with Christ, "that we may be also glorified together" (v. 17). The glory infinitely will outweigh the suffering (v. 18).

But the Bible does teach degrees of reward in heaven and punishment in hell (Matt. 25:14–30; Luke 19:12–27). All the regenerated will be saved in heaven. Some will be saved "as by fire" (1 Cor. 3:14–15); their useless works will be burned. Each will enjoy heaven to his or her full capacity. But that capacity will be determined by one's growth and service in and for Christ while on earth.

In the light of this threefold concept of salvation it is correct to say, "I am saved; I am being saved; I will be saved."

SOME QUESTIONS FOR FURTHER THOUGHT

1. Have you been saved? If so, how? Could you explain the plan of salvation to another person?

2. What is the threefold nature of salvation? Are you content merely to be regenerated? What is the meaning of full-redemption?

3. Explain "I am saved; I am being saved; I will be saved."

six

GOD'S PURPOSE OF GRACE

Election is the gracious purpose of God, according to which He regenerates, sanctifies, and glorifies sinners. It is consistent with the free agency of man, and comprehends all the means in connection with the end. It is a glorious display of God's sovereign goodness, and is infinitely wise, holy, and unchangeable. It excludes boasting and promotes humility.

All true believers endure to the end. Those whom God has accepted in Christ, and sanctified by His Spirit, will never fall away from the state of grace, but shall persevere to the end. Believers may fall into sin through neglect and temptation, whereby they grieve the Spirit, impair their graces and comforts, bring reproach on the cause of Christ, and temporal judgments on themselves, yet they shall be kept by the power of God through faith unto salvation.

Gen. 12:1–3; Ex. 19:5–8; 1 Sam. 8:4–7,19–22; Isa. 5:1–7; Jer. 31:31 ff.; Matt. 16:18–19; 21:28–45; 24:22,31; 25:34; Luke 1:68–79; 2:29–32; 19:41–44; 24:44–48; John 1:12–14; 3:16; 5:24; 6:44–45,65; 10:27–29; 15:16; 17:6,12,17–18; Acts 20:32; Rom. 5:9–10; 8:28–39; 10:12–15; 11:5–7,26–36; 1 Cor. 1:1–2; 15:24–28; Eph. 1:4–23; 2:1–10; 3:1–11; Col. 1:12–14; 2 Thess. 2:13–14; 2 Tim. 1:12; 2:10,19; Heb. 11:39 to 12:2; 1 Pet. 1:2–5,13; 2:4–10; 1 John 1:7–9; 2:19; 3:2

God's purpose of grace runs throughout the Bible. Indeed, the Scriptures teach that this redemptive purpose is from eternity. Before creation an omniscient God knew that man would sin and would need to be saved. However, God's foreknowledge of the event did not cause it. It came through the exercise of man's free will. Even so, knowing the event, in eternity God purposed to redeem men. Thus Christ is the Lamb slain from the foundation of the world. Therefore, forgiveness was in the heart of God before sin was in the heart of man. So God's purpose of grace refers to God's purpose fully to save man: regeneration, sanctification, and glorification. This purpose involves several things.

Election

Election is one of the great doctrines of the Bible. Yet the word itself does not appear in the Old Testament; it is found only in six verses in the New

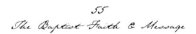

Testament (Rom 9:11; 11:5,7,28; 1 Thess. 1:4; 2 Pet. 1:10). But the word *elect* appears in the Old Testament and *elect* and *chosen* both appear in the New Testament.

There are certain pitfalls to be avoided in considering the doctrine of election. One should not magnify certain aspects of God's nature (sovereignty, will, power, pleasure) to the neglect of others (righteousness, love). Neither should one forget the free will of man and his power of choice. Also, election should not be regarded as God's purpose to save as few as possible rather than as many as possible. The tenor of the Bible is that God loves all men and wishes to save as many as possible. Again, it should not be viewed as relating to the saving of certain individuals to the neglect of all others. Such a position negates the abundant teachings of the Bible to the contrary. The pitfall resulting from these others is fatalism. If some are saved and others lost regardless of what they do or do not do, what incentive is there to seek the Lord or to preach the gospel? But the facts of Scripture are that man is not a puppet on a string. Election never appears in the Bible as mechanical or as blind destiny. It has to do with a God of love and with man who is morally responsible. Election never appears as a violation of the human will (Matt. 23:37–38). Note John 6:44. "No man can come to me, except the Father ... draw him." "Draw" is God's initiative. "Come" is man's response.

Two truths, therefore, must be recognized in regard to election: God's sovereignty and man's free will. Both are abundantly taught in the Bible.

In the abstract, God's sovereignty means that He can act as He wills without any outside counsel or permission. But in the concrete, as taught in the Bible, God has placed certain limitations upon Himself. In that sense His sovereignty must be viewed as His power to act as He wills in keeping with His own laws and according to His nature as righteousness and love.

On the other hand, the Bible teaches that man possesses a free will. God made him so. And while man is free to choose, he is responsible for his choices (Gen. 3; Rom. 1—3). This fact must be kept in mind as one considers the doctrine of election. Otherwise, man is not a free person capable of fellowship with God. And in the ultimate sense, God himself would be responsible for man's sinful acts.

Obviously, to finite intellects, it is impossible to harmonize God's sovereignty and man's free will. But in the infinite wisdom of God there is no conflict (Rom. 11:33–36). Perhaps at the human level an illustration will help. God in his sovereignty has ordained certain natural laws. But man is free to live by them or contrary to them. To be sure, he is left with the consequences. But he is still free to choose. The same is true of God's spiritual laws. Man can choose to live by them and be blessed, or he can do otherwise and be cursed. But God does not coerce in either event.

God proposed to save man. He took the initiative in doing so. Apart from God's initiative and saving purpose, man cannot be saved. The greatest thing

about man is not that he is seeking God but that God is seeking man (Luke 19:10).

This dual truth stands out in Ephesians 1:3–13, Paul's most complete treatment of election. Note the words "hath chosen" and "having predestinated" in verses 4–5. The former translates the Greek verb for *elect*. So God "elected us in him before the foundation of the world." "Predestinated" translates a verb meaning to mark out the boundaries beforehand (see v. 11). But note also that God has chosen "in him." Thus God's election was in Christ. And he marked out the boundaries of salvation in love, not by an arbitrary choice.

Against this background it is well to note that in eleven verses Paul used the phrase "in Christ" or its equivalent ten times. So God has chosen "in the sphere of Christ." He elected that all who are "in Christ" shall be saved. "In Christ" is the boundary that God marked out beforehand, like building a fence around a field. God did this in his sovereignty. he asked the counsel or permission of no one. All who are within the fence "in Christ" shall be saved.

Man is free to choose whether or not he will be in Christ. This does not mean that man can boast of his salvation once he chooses Christ. It is the result of God's initiative and saving purpose. Man receives this inheritance because God marked out the boundaries of salvation beforehand according to the counsel of his own will (v. 11). Thus it should be to his glory that men had a hope beforehand (v. 12) in Christ.

But at this point Paul took care of man's free will. It is seen in the passage "in whom also after that ye believed" (v. 13). Paul's readers heard the gospel of salvation that all who are "in Christ" shall be saved. They could have rejected it and remained in a lost condition. But they believed "in Christ" and thus were saved. That God knew beforehand who would believe is obvious. But, as previously stated, foreknowledge of an event does not cause it.

God never violates human personality. He will not save a man against his will. He knocks at the door of the heart, but He will not force it to open. However, to all who of their own wills will open the door, He enters and saves graciously apart from man's own efforts or merits.

It should be noted further that having elected a plan of salvation, God elected a people whereby that plan might be provided and propagated. This is seen in God's choice of Abraham and his descendants, and in the covenant which God made with Israel. Though Israel failed to keep that covenant, it was out of Israel that Jesus came to implement in history God's eternal redemptive purpose. And those who follow Him are a "chosen [elect] generation, a royal priesthood, an holy nation, a peculiar people; that ye should shew forth praises of him who hath called you out of darkness into his marvellous light: which in time past were not a people, but are now the people of God" (1 Pet. 2:9–10).

Mullins sums up all of this in his definition of election. "Election is not to be thought of as a bare choice of so many human units by God's action inde-

The Baptist Faith & Message

pendently of man's free choice and the human means employed. God elects men to respond freely. He elects to reach men through their native faculties and through the church, through evangelism and education and missionary endeavor. We must include all these elements in election. Otherwise we split the decree of God into parts and leave out an essential part."[1]

Stagg completes the picture. "One is strangely insensitive to the throb and pulse beat of the whole New Testament if he thinks that each man's fate is determined for him in advance. This is not a 'rigged' television show. God is not playing with toys or manipulating gadgets; he is seeking men who stand in awesome freedom where they may accept or reject the salvation which God alone can offer."[2]

Perseverance

Baptists believe that "all true believers endure to the end." But note that it is "true believers," not superficial ones. Many people believe about Jesus but not in him. But "those whom God has accepted in Christ, and sanctified by His Spirit, will never fall away from the state of grace, but shall persevere to the end."

Those who believe otherwise point to certain isolated passages or verses which they hold to teach to the contrary. No passage should be interpreted outside the context of the entire New Testament, whose overall teaching clearly declares the perseverance of the saints. Judas Iscariot is used as an example of one who fell away. But a study of his life shows that he never truly believed in Jesus as his Savior (John 6:70). Judas never called Jesus "Lord," only "Master" or rabbi or teacher.

Obviously, space does not permit a full treatment of all New Testament passages which teach the perseverance of the saints. But a few will suffice.

Jesus himself was speaking in John 10:28–29. Literally, "And I keep on giving to them age-abiding life, and not never [strong double negative] shall they be destroyed unto the age, and not anything [man, thing, or devil] shall snatch them out of my hand. My Father who has given [perfect tense, a completed work, past, present, future] to me is greater than all, and no one [nothing] is powerful to snatch out of the Father's hand." Believers do not hold on to God. In Christ he holds on to them.

In Colossians 3:3 Paul expresses the same idea in a different figure. "For ye are dead [ye died, to sin], and your [spiritual] life is hid [perfect tense, completely hid] with Christ in God." The verb rendered "is hid" carries the idea of a lock. The life of the believer is protected by a double lock: one is "with Christ," the other is "in God." To snatch away a believer, one would have to get by both. And no man, thing, or devil can do that.

The same figure is found in 2 Timothy 1:12. Here Paul used the figure of making a deposit in a bank. The Greek text reads, "For I know in whom I have fully believed, and am fully persuaded that he is able to guard my deposit unto that day."

The very nature of salvation assures perseverance. This is seen in Ephesians 2:8–10. Again reading from the Greek text: "For by grace have ye been saved through faith; and that not out of yourselves: it is the gift of God: not out of works, lest anyone should boast. For we are his workmanship, being created in the sphere of Christ Jesus for good works, which God has before ordained in order that in the sphere of them we should keep on walking about."

Salvation is a work of God's grace which the Christian receives through faith. Its source is neither one's self nor works. "Have ye been saved" means that it is a completed work wrought in the believer by God. So the Christian is a creation of God. Good works are not the root but the fruit of salvation. Since salvation is all of God in the beginning, its permanence is also all of God. So one's being saved and remaining so depends upon God and not upon one's self.

One of the greatest passages on the security of the believer is found in Ephesians 1:13–14. When one believes in Jesus Christ the Holy Spirit seals him as belonging to God. He is God's property, his "purchased possession." And the Holy Spirit indwelling him is "the earnest of our inheritance until the redemption [full redemption] of the purchased possession."

The Greek word rendered "earnest" may be translated variously: "installment" (Moffatt), "first installment" (Williams), "guarantee" (RSV), and "pledge" (Weymouth).

In the Greek papyri this word is often used in the sense of "earnest money," or a down payment which guarantees the full payment for the thing purchased. The "full redemption" suggests regeneration, sanctification, and glorification. The "purchased possession" is one's soul and Christian life, bought with the price of Jesus' atoning work (1 Cor. 6:20). The believer is both regenerated and sanctified by the work of the Holy Spirit. And his sealing and indwelling of the Christian is God's earnest money or guarantee that he will keep that soul and life looking toward the full redemption or glorification.

So God put up his earnest money, the Holy Spirit, as his guarantee that he would keep safe and fully redeem that which he has purchased. If one goes through with a transaction, his earnest money is a part of the purchase price. If he fails to complete the deal, he loses his earnest money. In Paul's example, the earnest money is the Holy Spirit. The Holy Spirit is God. So God has put up his very being as his guarantee to keep saved and to glorify the soul which believes in Jesus. If he failed even one soul in such a commitment, he would lose his earnest money, himself. He would cease to be. Thus so long as God is, so long is that soul safe which has leaned on Jesus for repose. One can ask for no better guarantee than this.

So much for the business transaction. There is a beautiful, romantic note in this word for earnest money. One papyri example of this word is that of "the engagement ring" as a pledge that one would go through with an agreement of marriage. So the Holy Spirit indwelling the Christian is Jesus' engagement ring which he places on the finger of his bride, looking toward the marriage feast of the Lamb (Rev. 21:2).

Personal Learning Activity 7

Pretend you are in a situation where you have to give evidence of why you believe in "once saved, always saved." Outline your arguments/proof with substantiating Scripture verses.

_____

_____

_____

_____

_____

The Christian and Sin

When you become a Christian, you are free from sin's penalty of death, but not from sin's power. So long as we are in the flesh, a civil war will rage within between carnal and spiritual natures. Paul describes his own struggle in Romans 7. His only assurance lies in "Jesus Christ our Lord" (v. 25). "There is therefore now no condemnation to them which are in Christ Jesus ["who walk not after the flesh, but after the Spirit" is not in the best manuscripts]. For the law of the Spirit of life in Christ Jesus hath made me free from the law of sin and death" (Rom. 8:1–2).

However, certain passages in 1 John are cited by some to show that the Christian does not sin, and that sin in one's life is proof that he is not a Christian. A case for such might be made from the *King James Version* if these passages are read in isolation. But a reading from the original Greek text shows that even these verses do not teach such. The verb tenses bring out the real meaning.

For instance, 1 John 3:8 reads, "He that committeth sin is of the devil." Here the verb is a present tense expressing continuous, repeated action or the habit of doing something. So, literally, "The one having the habit of doing sin is out of the devil." This means one who lives for the purpose of sinning. It is his whole life. Such a person is not a Christian.

Verse 9 reads, "Whosoever is born of God doth not commit sin; for his seed remaineth in him: and he cannot sin, because he is born of God." Here again the tenses are present. Literally, "Every one having been born out of God does not have the habit of doing sin; because his [God's] seed keeps on abiding in him: and he does not have the power to keep on sinning as a habit of life."

The person who is not a Christian lives for the purpose of sinning. He looks forward to it, and seeks out opportunity to do so. But the person who has been born of God has a new nature. He does not make sinning the habit of his life. Like Paul he may at times, under temptation, yield to his carnal nature. But he does not want to in his redeemed self. Having done so, he repents, asks forgiveness, and in God's power endeavors not to sin. God's seed abiding in him keeps him from having the habit of sinning.

Now look at other verses in 1 John. In 1:10 we read, "If we say that we have not sinned, we must make him [God] a liar, and his word is not in us." Here the verb is a perfect tense. It expresses completed action, covering past, present, and future. It refers here to one who says that he has never sinned in the past, does not sin now, and will not sin in the future. Obviously such a person makes God a liar when God says that all have sinned (Rom. 3:23). Such a person has no conviction of sin. He has never been a Christian. God's Word is not in him at all.

But notice verses 7–8. "The blood of Jesus Christ his Son cleanseth us from all sin. If we say that we have no sin, we deceive ourselves, and the truth is not in us." Here again are two present tenses. "If we say that we keep on not having sin, we keep on deceiving ourselves, and the truth is not in us." These words refer to the Christian. Though the blood of Jesus Christ keeps on cleansing us from sin, the Christian on occasion in weakness will commit sin. To think otherwise is self-deception.

But the glorious thing for the Christian is that "if we confess [keep on confessing] our sins, he is faithful and just to forgive us our sins, and to cleanse us from all unrighteousness" (v. 9). In this verse, "confess" is a present tense. It may be translated "confess from time to time" or when the Christian sins. When from time to time the Christian confesses sins, Christ most surely will forgive and cleanse from that sin. He does so on the basis of His blood shed for the sins of men (v. 7).

But this very fact should lead the Christian to endeavor to avoid sinning. For when he sins he grieves the Holy Spirit (Eph. 4:25–32). He brings shame on the cause of Christ, impairs his own usefulness as a Christian, mars his joy in Christ, and suffers the temporal consequences of his sins.

The Christian should beware of sins of omission as well as sins of commission. With his life founded upon Christ, he should not build a structure of useless works out of wood, hay, and stubble. Rather he should build out of gold, silver, and precious stones (1 Cor. 3:11–12). For "every man's work shall be made manifest: for the day [of judgment] shall declare it, because it shall

be revealed by fire; and the fire shall try every man's work of what sort it is. If any man's work abide which he hath built thereupon, he shall receive a reward. If any man's work shall be burned, he shall suffer loss: but he himself shall be saved; yet so as by fire" (1 Cor. 3:13–15). For his soul "shall be kept by the power of God through faith unto salvation."

SOME QUESTIONS FOR FURTHER THOUGHT

1. Is God's offer of salvation made to a select few, or is it made to all men? Is "election" arbitrary on God's part, or does it also involve the free will of man? Is it possible to harmonize God's sovereignty and man's free will? What is meant by God's election of a plan and a people?

2. What is the meaning of "perseverance of the saints"? Does this mean that all church members will be saved? Or all Baptists? Who does the saving and preserving of the saints or believers?

3. What is the relation of sin to the Christian's life? Does the security of the believer justify sin in his life? What does the Christian lose when he sins?

PEOPLE
OF THE FAITH

THE CHURCH
BAPTISM AND THE LORD'S SUPPER
THE LORD'S DAY

seven

THE CHURCH

A New Testament church of the Lord Jesus Christ is a local body of baptized believers who are associated by covenant in the faith and fellowship of the gospel, observing the two ordinances of Christ, committed to His teachings, exercising the gifts, rights, and privileges invested in them by His Word, and seeking to extend the gospel to the ends of the earth.

This church is an autonomous body, operating through democratic processes under the lordship of Jesus Christ. In such a congregation members are equally responsible. Its Scriptural officers are pastors and deacons.

The New Testament speaks also of the church as the body of Christ which includes all of the redeemed of all the ages.

Matt. 16:15–19; 18:15–20; Acts 2:41–42,47; 5:11–14; 6:3–6; 13:1–3; 14:23,27; 15:1–30; 16:5; 20:28; Rom. 1:7; 1 Cor. 1:2; 3:16; 5:4–5; 7:17; 9:13–14; 12; Eph. 1:22–23; 2:19–22; 3:8–11,21; 5:22–32; Phil. 1:1; Col. 1:18; 1 Tim. 3:1–15; 4:14; 1 Pet. 5:1–4; Rev. 2—3; 21:2–3

The New Testament speaks of the church as both the body and the bride of Christ. He is the Head of the body (Col. 1:18) and the Bridegroom of the bride (Matt. 9:15; Rev. 21:2). He both founded the church and purchased it with his blood. The church is the only institution founded by Christ. This he did that baptized believers might enjoy fellowship of faith and service in the gospel, observe the two ordinances, and through the exercise of their gifts received from the Holy Spirit extend the gospel throughout the earth.

Significance of the Word

The word "church" translates the Greek word *ekklesia* (note "ecclesiastic"). In turn, this word is composed of two other Greek words, *ek*, out of, and *kalein*, to call. Hence the meaning is "the called out ones" or "assembly."

Prior to the New Testament, the word had two general uses. In secular Greek it was used to designate the assembly of the citizens of a self-governing Greek city (Acts 19:39–41). Ephesus was granted the privilege of self-rule, but within the framework of the laws of the Roman Empire. In this sense an *ekklesia* was a local assembly operating through democratic processes under the laws of the Empire.

In the Septuagint, the Greek translation of the Old Testament, this word translated the Hebrew word *qahal*, referring to the nation of Israel assembled before God and under his direct theocratic rule (Deut. 31:30, congregation; Judges 21:8, assembly.)[1] Two uses are found in the New Testament (Acts 7:38; Heb. 2:12).

The word "church" in the New Testament never refers to organized Christianity or to a group of churches. It denotes either a local body of baptized believers or includes all the redeemed through all the ages. The greater emphasis among Baptists, as in the New Testament, is on the local church.[2]

Personal Learning Activity 8

Look up the following verses of Scripture and list the different words or phrases used to define the church: Ephesians 4:11–12; Acts 11:26; Revelation 19:7–10; 1 Peter 2:9–10; 1 Peter 5:2; 1 Corinthians 3:9; Ephesians 2:19; 2 Corinthians 6:16; Ephesians 2:22.

_____

_____

_____

Which of these definitions is your favorite? Why?_____

_____

_____

_____

Jesus and the Church

According to the Gospel records, Jesus used the word "church" only three times (Matt. 16:18; 18:17). The latter dealt with church discipline. The former was in his statement of purpose to build the church. Certainly the former, and probably the latter, speaks of the church in the institutional sense. He had no one particular church in mind, even though the truths declared may apply to any church. But certainly his teachings implied the church in a sense of a Christian fellowship (John 17:21).

Near Caesarea Philippi, following Peter's confession of Jesus as "the Christ, the Son of the living God" (Matt. 16:16), Jesus said, "Thou art Peter [petros], and upon this rock [petra] I will build my church; and the gates of hell shall not prevail against it."

It is not within the scope of this work to dwell long on the matter "Peter" (*petros*) and "rock" (*petra*).[3] It is sufficient to say that since *petros* is masculine and *petra* is feminine it is unlikely that the two are identical. A *petra* was a large ledge rock such as a foundation rock. A *petros* was a small stone broken off the large stone and partaking of its nature. Some scholars discount this distinction, holding that Jesus probably spoke in Hebrew or Aramaic, where such a distinction is absent. No one knows the language used. It could have been either of these or Greek. However, it is most likely that Matthew, in the Greek text, preserved the sense of Jesus' statement. In the Old Testament where "rock" is used symbolically, it always refers to deity.

Certainly the foundation of the church is Christ, not Peter or any other mere man (1 Cor. 3:11). There are varying views, even among Baptists, as to the meaning of Jesus' words. The writer sees "rock" as referring to Christ. Peter was a *petros*, a small stone partaking of Christ's nature. The church is built upon Christ, the building stones being all who, like Peter, confess him as "the Christ, the Son of the Living God." (See 1 Pet. 2:5.)

Perhaps scholars have spent so much time on this problem that they have missed the very point of Jesus' words. In the Greek text the emphasis is not on "Peter" or "rock" but on "my church." The disciples were aware of the dual use of *ekklesia* in the Greek and Hebrew sense. So, in effect, Jesus said, "The Greeks have *their* church, and the Hebrews have *their* church. Now I will build *my* church."

In this emphasis one sees the twofold nature of the church. On the one hand, the church is general in nature. It consists of all the redeemed of all the ages under the direct theocratic rule of God. On the other hand, there is the local church acting democratically, autonomously under the lordship of Jesus Christ.

To many Baptists, autonomy has become anarchy. This is true when either a church or an individual Baptist says, "I can do as I please!" Both should do as Christ pleases or wills. Either the word "autonomy" should be purged of such a meaning or a new word should be used. It is far more accurate and scriptural to say that a New Testament church is a local church acting through democratic processes under the lordship of Jesus Christ.

In such a church each member has equal rights and privileges but also should share equally the responsibilities. The will of the body should be the will of all, a will reached under the authority and guidance of the Spirit of Christ.

"And the gates of hell shall not prevail against it" (Matt. 16:18). This is often interpreted to mean that hell or evil will not overcome or stand up against the church. The idea is true. But this is not what Jesus said here. The Greek text reads, "And the gates of hades shall not have strength against it." Hades is the abode of the dead. Gates are used either to keep out or to keep in. Those outside hades are not trying to get in; those inside are trying to get out. These gates shall not be able to hold Christ's people in the abode of the dead. So this is a promise of the resurrection. Christ's church shall live on after physical death.

Mission of the Church

In Ephesians 3:10–11 Paul said that the eternal purpose of God in Christ is to be declared "by" or "through the church." So the church stands at the center of God's redemptive purpose in Christ. The church in the general sense is made up of those redeemed through Christ. The local church is composed of baptized believers. The mission of both is to declare the gospel of redemption to a lost world.

Returning to Jesus' words in Matthew 16, one reads, "And I will give unto thee the keys of the kingdom of heaven: and whatsoever thou shalt bind on earth shall be bound in heaven: and whatsoever thou shalt loose on earth shall be loosed in heaven" (v. 19). Roman Catholics interpret this verse as the basis of papal authority. To them the keys are political and spiritual respectively. They relate binding and loosing to retaining or forgiving sin. Baptists reject this interpretation. Catholics insist that these words were spoken to Peter alone, since "to thee" (*soi*) is a singular pronoun. However, Peter spoke to Jesus for the twelve (v. 16) and Jesus spoke to the twelve through Peter. Jesus used these same words in connection with the church or a church (Matt. 18:18).

The writer sees verse 19 as spoken to the twelve as representative of the church fellowship. "Keys" are for opening or locking doors. So these keys either open the doors to the kingdom of heaven or lock the same.

Perhaps a literal translation of verse 19 will prove helpful. It reads "shall have been bound ... shall have been loosed." The keys of the kingdom are the gospel which Jesus deposited in his church. If the church binds it on earth by not proclaiming it, heaven has already decreed that there is no other way whereby men may be saved and enter into the kingdom of heaven. But if the church looses the gospel on earth by proclaiming it, heaven has already decreed that men will hear it, some will believe it, and those who do will be saved or enter into the kingdom of heaven. It is a privilege and a tremendous responsibility!

It is in this light that one may understand Jesus' commissions to evangelize the world (Matt. 28:18–20; Luke 24:44–49; John 20:21–23; Acts 1:8). This is the meaning of 1 Peter 2:4–10. The church is the true Israel of God. The letter to the Hebrews may be seen in this light as a call to world missions. This is the sense of Revelation 22:17.

Moffatt translates Philippians 3:20, "But we are a colony of heaven." Under the Roman system, certain cities were rewarded for faithful service by being made colonies. They not only guarded and policed their surrounding area, but

their citizens so lived as to cause others to desire to become Romans. They were little bits of Rome set down in the Empire.

So Paul said that as Philippi was such a colony, so the church there was a colony of heaven. It was a little bit of heaven set down in a pagan world. Its citizens were to permeate its environment with the principles of heaven. And each member should so live as to cause all others to wish to become citizens of God's kingdom. This may be said of every local church.

The Church and the Kingdom

Various views are held regarding the kingdom. Some distinguish between the kingdom of God and the kingdom of heaven. However, it should be noted that the Gospel writers do not seem to make such a distinction. In reporting the same teaching of Jesus the terms are used interchangeably (Matt. 13:11,31; Mark 4:11,30; Luke 8:10). Note that Mark and Luke used "kingdom of God," and Matthew used "kingdom of heaven."

In the broader sense the kingdom of God is the reign of God in his universe. He rules over all created things: angels, men, devils, nature. The church, therefore, is one phase of that kingdom. The church general, as composed of all the redeemed, is in the kingdom of God. The local church is an earthly colony of that kingdom. Following the Lord's return and the judgment, God will reign over a redeemed creation (1 Cor. 15:24–28); over Satan, his angels, and the unregenerate in hell (Rev. 20:10–15); and in heaven over the holy angels and the redeemed of all the ages (Rev. 21—22).

Jesus came to establish the reign of God not only in people's hearts but over all things in the universe. He proved Satan's claim to sovereignty to be false. Each soul submitting to God through Christ enters the kingdom by willingly accepting God's rule and thus becomes a part of the church general. Believer's baptism then is required to become a part of the fellowship of the local church. Distinction may be made between the church and the kingdom by seeing the church, general and local, as that phase of God's kingdom charged with the extension of God's rule in people's hearts. To the church, and to no other institution, are given the keys of the kingdom.

Whereas one is born again into the church general, one becomes a part of a local church through believer's baptism. To the local church Jesus committed the ordinances of baptism and the Lord's Supper that in their observance the church might witness to his saving work in its locality. Thus while salvation is synonymous with membership in the church general, it is not true with regard to local church membership. Nor is membership in the local church synonymous with salvation. "Fellowship," not "membership," is the New Testament word for Christian relations in the local church.

In the New Testament the greater emphasis is upon the local church. Of 115 times *ekklesia* appears in the New Testament, 93 refer to the local church.

Note "the church of God which is at Corinth" (1 Cor. 1:2; 2 Cor. 1:1) and "the churches of Galatia" (Gal. 1:2). The local church is the visible operation of the church general in a given time and place. As such the local church is a democratic body under the lordship of Christ directing its own affairs: selecting deacons (Acts 6:1–6), administering the ordinances (Acts 2:41–42), approving the work of evangelism (Acts 11:1–18), sending out missionaries and receiving their reports (Acts 13—14), and administering church discipline (1 Cor. 5:1–5).

Each New Testament church was a separate unit, exercising no authority over other churches and not being ruled by any other church or Christian body. But while independent, by common consent they cooperated in matters of mutual concern, such as doctrine and aid to other churches. Baptists are an independent people who exercise their independence through voluntary cooperation.

Officers of the Local Church

The officers in a local New Testament church are pastors and deacons (Phil. 1:1). The same office is variously called bishop, elder, or pastor. The qualification for pastors and deacons are set forth in 1 Timothy 3 (on deacons see also Acts 6:3).

"Bishop" comes from the Greek word for overseer, one who oversaw the work of others that it might be done correctly. "Elder" translates the Greek word which connotes age. Among the Jews it was used of one who because of age possessed dignity and wisdom. But in the Christian sense it was used of those who presided over assemblies of the church. This suggests the leaders in the church. The very name connotes the office of counselor. "Pastor" renders the word for shepherd or one who feeds and tends the flock.

That these three words refer to the same office is seen in Acts 20:28. These words were spoken to the elders of the church in Ephesus (v. 17). Note "overseers" and "to feed [as a shepherd] the church of God." Titus 1:5–6 uses "elder" and "bishop" interchangeably. And in Acts 20:28 "to feed as a shepherd" completes the picture of these words for the same office. In the New Testament, "bishop" never refers to one over a group of churches. And "elder" in the Christian sense always refers to the same office of bishop or pastor.

While the word "deacon" does not appear in Acts 6:1–8, this passage probably refers to the origin of the office. The Greek word means one who serves, actually a menial servant or a slave. Both Jesus and Paul saw themselves as such servants (Matt. 20:28; Col 1:25). "False prophets" were called Satan's deacons (2 Cor. 11:15).

Deacons served in both material and spiritual matters (Acts 6:2 to 7:60; 8:5–40). Stephen, the first Christian martyr, was a deacon. Philip also is called an "evangelist" (Acts 21:8). Note that when both pastors and deacons did their work faithfully, the work of the church prospered (Acts 6:7).

That there are two ordained offices does not mean that a church may not have other workers, such as teachers and leaders, in various phases of the work. Such may be chosen as the need demands. But the ordained officers are pastors and deacons.

Personal Learning Activity 8

Define the following biblical words that apply to the office or position of pastor.

Bishop _____

_____

Elder _____

_____

Pastor _____

_____

What is the meaning of the word that is translated *deacon* in the New Testament?

_____

_____

Center of Labor and Loyalty

Since God's eternal redemptive purpose is to be realized "through the church" (Eph. 3:10–11), participation in this purpose should be the center of the Christian's labor and loyalty. And since in this age that center is the local church, the Christian's labor and loyalty should be through the local church fellowship of which he is a part.

There are many worthy causes and institutions through which one may labor in the community. But this should not be done at the expense of one's responsibility in and through one's church. The good must not become the enemy of the best.

Billy Graham and I were playing golf. I said, "Billy, I wish God would raise up a thousand like you. We need them and crusades such as yours. But I still believe that in the main God's redemptive purpose runs through His local churches." He replied: "The next time you say that will you quote me as having said it? Without the local churches I am dead."

He holds crusades only upon invitation of local churches in a given area. Even then they are local churches of various persuasions cooperating under his leadership in the common cause of evangelism.

Men may look askance upon the church. But it is still the body and bride of Christ through which he has chosen to do his work. If the Christian wants to be where the action is, he should invest his life for Christ in and through the church.

SOME QUESTIONS FOR FURTHER THOUGHT

1. What is the meaning of the word "church"? What is the purpose and function of the church?

2. Study the meaning of "my church" in Matthew 16:18. What does it teach as to the nature of the church? What is the meaning of "theocracy" and "democracy" with respect to the church? How may the word "autonomy" be abused?

3. What is the relationship between the church and the kingdom of God?

4. Is the local church of which you are a member the center of your loyalty and service? If not, why not?

eight
BAPTISM AND THE LORD'S SUPPER

Christian baptism is the immersion of a believer in water in the name of the Father, the Son, and the Holy Spirit. It is an act of obedience symbolizing the believer's faith in a crucified, buried, and risen Savior, the believer's death to sin, the burial of the old life, and the resurrection to walk in newness of life in Christ Jesus. It is a testimony to his faith in the final resurrection of the dead. Being a church ordinance, it is prerequisite to the privileges of church membership and to the Lord's Supper.
The Lord's Supper is a symbolic act of obedience whereby members of the church, through partaking of the bread and the fruit of the vine, memorialize the death of the Redeemer and anticipate His second coming.

Matt. 3:13–17; 26:26–30; 28:19–20; Mark 1:9–11; 14:22–26; Luke 3:21–22; 22:19–20; John 3:23; Acts 2:41–42; 8:35–39; 16:30–33; Acts 20:7; Rom. 6:3–5; 1 Cor. 10:16,21; 11:23–29; Col. 2:12.

The New Testament church had two ordinances: baptism and the Lord's Supper, and in that order (Acts 2:41–42). Both are symbolic, not sacramental, in meaning.

The word "ordinance" is never used in the New Testament in direct reference to baptism or the Lord's Supper. Various words in both Testaments are translated "ordinance," but they have reference to laws, judgments, or decrees. The word translated "ordinances" in 1 Corinthians 11:2 means "traditions," or things handed down. In this case it refers to teachings declared by Paul to the Corinthian Christians. The word *ordinance* basically means a decree or command. In this sense it is used of baptism and the Lord's Supper whose observance by his followers was commanded by Jesus (Matt. 28:19; Luke 22:19; 1 Cor. 11:23–26). They symbolize what Jesus did for one's salvation, what he does in the believer, and faith in the Lord's return and its meaning.

Baptism

The word *baptism* comes from the Greek word *baptizō* which means to dip, plunge, submerge, or immerse. In classical Greek it was used of dipping animals or of the sinking of a ship. In the Septuagint it is used of Naaman dipping himself in the Jordan (2 Kings 5:14).

The New Testament used the word in several ways: submerging the body or hands in water (Mark 7:4; Luke 11:38); being overwhelmed or submerged in trouble (Matt. 20:22–23; Mark 10:38–39); and performing the ceremony of baptism.

Baptism in the New Testament was related to the ministry of both John the Baptist and Jesus. John's baptism was symbolic of one's repentance from sin and of willingness to participate in the kingdom of God (Matt. 3:6–8; Luke 3:3–16). Jesus submitted to John's baptism (Matt. 3:16) not to denote repentance but to authenticate John's ministry, to set an example for his followers, and to dedicate himself publicly to his redemptive ministry. In it Jesus symbolized his death, burial, and resurrection. Thus it was a transition from John's baptism to Christian baptism. Acts 19:1–5 clearly shows a distinction between the two baptisms.

At this point it is well to note the two noun forms denoting baptism. One is *baptismos*, referring to the act itself. It is used only three times in the New Testament and never with regard to Christian baptism (Mark 7:4, "washing" not genuine in v. 8; Heb. 6:2; 9:10). The other word is *baptisma*, connoting the meaning in the act. It is found twenty-two times in the New Testament. Except for Hebrews 6:2, "baptism" renders *baptisma*.

In 1 Peter 3:20–21 Peter speaks of Noah's family being saved "by water. The like figure whereunto even baptism doth also now save us." The Greek reads *dia hundatos* or "through water." They were not saved by being in the water. They were saved (rescued) through the flood by being in the ark, a type of Christ.

"Baptism" translates *baptisma*, the meaning in the act of baptism, namely, a symbol of what Jesus did to save us—death, burial, and resurrection. And what He does in the believer—death to the old life, its burial, and resurrection to a new life in Christ.

Baptisma is not found in any Greek writing except the New Testament and later Christian writings. It seems that the Holy Spirit coined this word to express the symbolic nature of baptism.

Keeping in mind the meaning of *baptisma*, what is the significance of Christian baptism? Is it sacramental in nature and necessary for salvation, or is it symbolic in nature? The word itself strongly suggests the latter. The idea of baptismal regeneration did not appear in Christian teachings until late in the second and early in the third centuries. In the first century certain heretical teachers sought to inject something other than grace through faith into the plan of salvation (Acts 15; Gal. 2; Col. 2:16–23). But all these were rejected by the early Christians.

However, by the late second and early third centuries, baptismal regeneration came to be accepted by the group which later evolved into the Roman Catholic Church. Happily, however, there persisted a minority, usually underground, which held to the New Testament faith. Today the idea of sacramen-

The Baptist Faith & Message

tal baptism persists in Catholicism and to a degree in most branches of Protestantism.

Certain proof passages are cited in this regard. But when these passages are seen in their proper light, the proof disappears. No one verse or passage should be interpreted contrary to the overall teaching of the New Testament. And the New Testament abundantly teaches salvation apart from baptism (Luke 13:3,5; 15:7; John 3:16–18; 5:24; Acts 16:30–31; Rom. 10:8–10; Eph. 1:13–14; 2:8–10; 1 Pet. 1:18–23; 1 John 5:10–12).

But what about these proof passages? "Except a man be born of water and of the Spirit, he cannot enter into the kingdom of God" (John 3:5). Certainly the much disputed meaning of "of water" makes this a shaky basis for baptismal regeneration. Its absence from verses 3, 7, and 16 strongly argues against this position. This probably corresponds to "born of the flesh" in verse 6.[1]

What about Mark 16:16? It is sufficient to say that the best manuscripts of Mark end with 16:8. So in all likelihood verses 9–20 are not genuine. Note the absence of "is baptized" in the last part of verse 16. This is the same passage that teaches snake-handling and poison-drinking as proof of one's faith (v. 18). By his own action, Jesus forbade such dangerous acts (Matt. 4:5–7). Rejecting Mark 16:9–20 loses no truth taught in the other Gospels. It does dispel certain things which are contrary to overall Christian truth.[2]

"Repent, and be baptized ... for the remission of sins" (Acts 2:38). The interpretation of this verse hinges on the word "for" (eis). Eis may be translated "for," "unto," "into," "because of," "on the basis of," "with respect to," "with reference to," or "as the result of." It depends upon the context, which in this case is the entire New Testament. In Matthew 12:41 and Luke 11:32 it is rendered "at." The men of Nineveh repented at the preaching of Jonas. They repented not that Jonah might preach, but as the result of his preaching. Here it definitely is result, not purpose. Even the English word "for" may carry this meaning. "He was executed for murder." Not that he might murder, but because he had already murdered.

So it makes good sense to read, "Repent and be baptized [as the result of or on the basis of] the remission of sins." And this corresponds to the broad teachings of the New Testament concerning baptism. Worthy of note is the fact that Jesus did all that was necessary for man's salvation. Yet he baptized no one (John 4:2). Paul was the apostle to the Gentiles. Still he plainly stated that he was sent to preach the gospel, not to baptize (1 Cor. 1:14–17).

That immersion is the original form of baptism is generally agreed. *Baptizō* itself teaches that neither pouring nor sprinkling constitutes New Testament baptism. Because of the later belief in baptismal regeneration, the practice arose of pouring water all over a sick person. This was called clinical baptism. Later, water was poured only on the head. It should be noted that while the verbs for "pour" and "sprinkle" appear in the New Testament, neither is used for baptism. No usage has been found where *baptizō* means either pour or sprinkle. The practice of sprinkling for baptism gradually replaced immersion in the Catholic Church and when it divided into the Roman and Greek branches, the latter retained immersion. It was not until the thirteenth century that sprinkling became the official mode of Roman Catholic baptism.

In Florence, Italy, one may still see the Baptistery, dating back to the eleventh century. It was the place for baptism. Dante was immersed here. In the center of this building is a large baptistry. Built into its top at one corner is a smaller baptistry where babies were immersed. On the wall of this building is a large mural depicting John immersing Jesus in the Jordan. Catholic churches in Europe which were built prior to the thirteenth century, and which have murals or mosaics showing Jesus' baptism, show him being immersed. The Roman Catholics admit that they simply changed the mode. The change in mode came after the change in meaning.

Baptists, on the basis of clear New Testament evidence, reject both changes. Baptism is for believers only, symbolizing but not in any sense causing salvation. Obviously they reject infant baptism. New Testament baptism, while unnecessary for salvation, is to be administered only to those who have made a conscious committal to Jesus Christ through a personal faith in him.

Why Baptists reject sprinkling and pouring for baptism is quite clear. The mode is not New Testament baptism, and back of it is a perversion of the meaning. But why do Baptists reject the baptism of those who practice immersion for salvation? The same principle applies.

Assuming a believer as the subject, New Testament baptism requires both a proper meaning and a proper mode to express that meaning. The meaning is a symbol of Christ's redeeming work for and in the believer. Only immersion expresses that meaning. But even though a group may use the proper mode, if the meaning be sacramental it is still not New Testament baptism. Change the mode and the meaning is lost. Change the meaning and the mode loses its New Testament significance.

Baptism is not necessary for being in the kingdom of God or the church general. But it is necessary for fellowship in the local church. "Being a church ordinance, it is prerequisite to the privileges of church membership and to the Lord's Supper."

Personal Learning Activity 9

What would you say to an adult who has recently accepted Christ as His personal Savior but does not want to be baptized? Write some key words you would use to try to show him the importance of baptism.

The Baptist Faith & Message

Lord's Supper

The Lord's Supper is the other church ordinance (Matt. 26:26–29; Mark 14:22–25; Luke 22:17–20; 1 Cor. 11:23–26). A study of the Gospel passages in context reveals that Judas left the upper room prior to the instituting of the Supper. The Supper is for baptized believers only. Doubtless Judas had been baptized, but he was not a believer.

The elements used in the Supper were unleavened bread and "the fruit of the vine." The word "wine" is not used. Some interpret "fruit of the vine" as wine. However, as the bread was unleavened, free of bacteria, was the cup also not grape juice? Wine is the product of the juice plus fermentation caused by bacteria. Since both elements represented the pure body and blood of Jesus, there is reason to ponder. The writer sees "fruit of the vine" as pure grape juice untainted by fermentation.

Four views have been held historically with regard to the Lord's Supper. Roman Catholics believe in transubstantiation, or that the elements in the Mass actually become the body and blood of Jesus. Lutherans believe in consubstantiation, a modification of the Roman Catholic view. In this view, the body and blood of jesus are present with the elements. Some other denominations believe in the Lord's Supper as a means of grace. Discounting the above views, they hold that one receives grace by partaking of the Supper. All of these are sacramentarian in degree. Baptists believe that the elements merely symbolize the body and blood of Jesus, with no saving effect in partaking of them.

When Jesus said, "This is my body" and "this is my blood" (Matt. 26:26,28), he no more meant that they actually became such than by saying, "I am the door" (John 10:9), he meant that he was a hole in a wall or a piece of wood. In all cases he spoke symbolically. So the elements are merely symbols of his body and blood. Like the meaning in baptism, the elements portray that which Jesus did for believers' salvation. Both are visual aids whereby believers portray the basis and experience of their saving relationship with Jesus Christ.

Jesus did not say when or how often believers should observe the Lord's Supper. He instituted it on Thursday night. New Testament Christians observed it on the Lord's Day. Jesus did say that "as often as ye eat this bread, and drink this cup, ye do shew [proclaim] the lord's death till he come" (1 Cor. 11:26). Both bread and cup are to be taken "in remembrance of me [Jesus]" (1 Cor. 11:24–25). Both baptism and the Lord's Supper look back to

what Jesus has done in salvation and forward to His glorious second coming.

Both ordinances are sermons in symbol of Jesus' redeeming work and promised return. Baptism is an initiatory ordinance to be administered to the believer only one time. The Lord's Supper is a continuing ordinance to be observed at stated intervals throughout the believer's life until Jesus comes again.

New Testament baptized believers are eligible to take the Lord's Supper. Some Baptist churches hold that one should be a member of the church in which he partakes of it, holding that he should be in the fellowship and under the discipline of the church which administers it (1 Cor. 11:20–34). Many Baptist churches hold that any member of any Baptist church is eligible. Many others invite *all* true believers to participate at the Lord's table.

Who is worthy to take part in the Supper? None, except by God's grace. "Unworthily" in 1 Corinthians 11:29 is an adverb of manner, referring to the manner in which one partakes of the Supper. The Lord's Supper should be a time of self-examination and reconsecration to Jesus Christ.

A brief word should be said about the charge that Baptists are "closed communionists." To begin with, the Lord's Supper is not communion between men but between the believer and the Lord. The word "communion" is used only one time with reference to the Lord's Supper (1 Cor. 10:16). The reference here (1 Cor. 10:16–33) is to the believer eating meat offered to idols. Paul was thinking of the Christian's union with Christ.

All Christian groups which practice baptism hold that it should precede the Lord's Supper. Baptists say the same thing. The question is, What constitutes New Testament baptism? Thus the difference between Baptists and others is at this point, not about the Supper. Therefore, if Baptists are "closed" anything they are "closed-baptismists"!

Since both baptism and the Lord's Supper are given as ordinances or commands of Jesus, both should be observed by every believer. Failure to do so is to be disobedient to the Lord's will.

Personal Learning Activity 10

Read the statements below very carefully. Place a T beside the statements that you believe are true. Place an F beside the statements that are false.

1.___ Baptists believe that baptism and the Lord's Supper are sacraments with saving power.

2.___ Baptism is a symbol of the death, burial, and resurrection of Jesus, as well as a symbol of our new life in Him.

3.___ The meaning of baptism can be conveyed through immersion, sprinkling, or pouring.

4.__ The Lord's Supper is a memorial of the suffering of Jesus.

5.__ Any person who wishes to do so is invited to observe the Lord's Supper.

6.__ Baptists consider baptism and the Lord's Supper to be *ordinances* rather than *sacraments*.

(*Answers:* 1–F; 2–T; 3–F; 4–T; 5–F; 6–T)

SOME QUESTIONS FOR FURTHER THOUGHT

1. What is the meaning of the word ordinance? Are the ordinances sacramentarian or symbolic in nature? What is the difference between these two ideas? What do baptism and the Lord's Supper symbolize?

2. What is your church's position regarding participants in its observance of the Lord's Supper?

3. Are Baptists "closed communionists" or "closed baptismists"? What is the difference between these terms?

nine

THE LORD'S DAY

The first day of the week is the Lord's Day. It is a Christian institution for regular observance. It commemorates the resurrection of Christ from the dead and should be employed in exercises of worship and spiritual devotion, both public and private, and by refraining from worldly amusements, and resting from secular employments, work of necessity and mercy only being excepted.

Ex. 20:8–11; Matt. 12:1–12; 28:1 ff.; Mark 2:27–28; 16:1–7; Luke 24:1–3,33-36; John 4:21–24; 20:1,19–28; Acts 20:7; 1 Cor. 16:1–2; Col. 2:16; 3:16; Rev. 1:10

In the Old Testament the seventh day of the week was set apart as the sabbath day (Ex. 20:8–11). The word "sabbath" means rest. So "sabbath" refers primarily to the purpose—not to the number—of the day. One day out of seven was to be a rest day.

The number of the day came from the fact that on the seventh day God rested from His creative work. Thus the Sabbath day, in addition to being a rest day, commemorated the finish of the work of God in creation. It was, therefore, a sacred day.

In the Gospels, Jesus and His disciples observed the seventh day as the Sabbath. They were Jews, and that was their day of rest and worship. It was designed to replenish both body and spirit.

By the time of Jesus, the Jewish religious teachers had devised more than fifteen hundred rules of conduct designed to regulate Sabbath observance. Thus the day had become more of a burden than a blessing. Jesus ignored these rules, but He never broke the Fourth Commandment as God intended it to be observed.

In Judaism there were four centers of emphasis: the Temple, the Scriptures, the traditions, and the Sabbath. Other religions had the first three. Only the Sabbath was peculiar to Judaism. Therefore, the Jewish religious leaders were unusually sensitive at this point. Because Jesus disregarded their many regulations, He was constantly in conflict with them over the observance of the Sabbath (Matt. 12:1–14; Mark 2:23—3:6; Luke 6:1–11; John 5:1–47).

Jesus' position was that "the sabbath was made for man, and not man for the sabbath: therefore the Son of man is Lord also of the sabbath" (Mark 2:27–28). The Sabbath day was to be a blessing, not a burden. Jesus set the day in its proper place in God's purpose. He taught three things to be done on the Sabbath: deeds of necessity, mercy, and worship (Matt. 12:3–5,9–13).

Early Christians were Jews who worshiped in the synagogue and Temple with other Jews. Paul and Barnabas went to the synagogues on that day because they found an audience to which they could preach the gospel.

The Seventh-Day Baptists today observe the seventh day for worship. Otherwise, along with other Christian groups, Baptists observe the first day.

Lord's Day

The term "Lord's Day" appears only one time in the New Testament (Rev. 1:10). While not stated, this most likely was the first day of the week.

There is no specific command in the New Testament to change from the seventh to the first day. However, it is evident that the first day of the week was observed by the early Christians following Jesus' resurrection. Wherever Christians as such were found gathered in worship, it was on the first day of the week (Acts 20:7; 1 Cor. 16:2).

Champions of the seventh day point out that Sunday was originally a pagan day set aside to the sun and its worship. However, the word "Sunday" is not used in the New Testament. It is "the first day of the week." The fact that this day was Sunday is secondary. The "first day of the week" is grounded in Christian, not pagan, practice.

As the seventh-day Sabbath commemorated God's completion of creation, so the Lord's Day commemorates His completion of His redemptive work. Jesus was raised from the dead on the first day of the week. It was natural, therefore, that His disciples gathered on that day to hear and share reports about the risen Lord. Twice Jesus appeared to the assembled group on succeeding first days of the week (John 20:19,26). His appearance on resurrection Sunday night would be natural. But why did He wait until the succeeding first day to appear again? It is possible that He did so to encourage His followers to set apart this day to assemble for worship.

The term "lord's Day" means a day belonging to the Lord. At one time this was regarded as a purely Christian term. But discoveries have shown that the Romans used the term to denote days set apart to honor the emperor. This custom throws light on the one use of the term in the New Testament. Revelation was written probably during the reign of Domitian (a.d. 81-96). Christians were being persecuted because they refused to say, "Caesar is Lord." Rather they said, "Jesus is Lord" (Rom. 10:9; 1 Cor. 12:3). It is possible that in protest to Caesar-worship the Christians adopted this term to denote the day on which they commemorated the Lord's resurrection. For it was by that event that Jesus was revealed fully and truly as Lord.

What relation may one see between the Hebrew Sabbath and the Christian Lord's Day? Since "Sabbath" means rest, in that sense they are related. The one commemorates God's rest from His creative work; the other celebrates that He rested from or completed His redemptive work.

It is at this point that they also differ. The Hebrew Sabbath was a recognition; the Lord's Day is a celebration. It is a day when believers worship God not as Creator alone but as Redeemer.

Certainly the Lord's Day should be one when believers rest from all unnecessary secular labors. Jesus' teaching about the Sabbath may well apply here: doing only deeds of mercy, necessity, and worship. The fact that the day was made for man and not man for the day does not permit its abuse by Christians as it is abused by non-Christians. It should be a day devoted to rest and worship.

But Stagg is right in drawing a distinction between the Lord's Day and the Hebrew Sabbath as such. "The sabbath was a day of rest from work. The Lord's Day has its true meaning in its positive emphasis, memorializing the resurrection of Christ. The day can have Christian meaning to those alone who know the risen Christ. The day is best observed by assembly, worship, and witnessing to the risen Christ. ... The hope for giving the day its Christian meaning is in Christ's becoming so real in his presence with us today that we will be moved by the same impulse which brought together an excited band of early believers, thrilled to proclaim, " 'It is the Lord! He is risen!' "[1]

Personal Learning Activity 11

The Lord's Day is a day "belonging to the Lord." It should be a day devoted to rest and worship. With these truths in mind, answer the following questions.

1. How does your observance of the Lord's Day reflect the fact that the day belongs to the Lord?

_____

_____

2. What are you doing in your observance of the Lord's Day that fulfills the purposes of worship and rest?

_____

_____

3. What changes could you make in the way you observe the Lord's Day that would improve your observance of His day?

_____

_____

SOME QUESTIONS FOR FURTHER THOUGHT

1. What is the meaning of the word *Sabbath*? How did it come to be associated with the seventh day? Which is more important—the number or the purpose of the day?

2. Why do most Christians observe the first day of the week? What is the difference in meaning between the "Sabbath Day" and the "Lord's Day"?

3. What did Jesus mean when He said that the Sabbath was made for man rather than man for the sabbath? Does this justify a wide-open Sunday? What deeds did Jesus teach that could be done on this day? How does this teaching relate to our complex age?

FULFILLMENT OF THE FAITH

THE KINGDOM

LAST THINGS

ten

THE KINGDOM

The Kingdom of God includes both His general sovereignty over the universe and His particular kingship over men who willfully acknowledge Him as King. Particularly the Kingdom is the realm of salvation into which men enter by trustful, childlike commitment to Jesus Christ. Christians ought to pray and to labor that the Kingdom may come and God's will be done on earth. The full consummation of the Kingdom awaits the return of Jesus Christ and the end of this age.

Gen. 1:1; Isa. 9:6–7; Jer. 23:5–6; Matt. 3:2; 4:8–10,23; 12:25–28; 13:1–52; 25:31–46; 26:29; Mark 1:14–15; 9:1; Luke 4:43; 8:1; 9:2; 12:31–32; 17:20–21; 23:42; John 3:3; 18:36; Acts 1:6–7; 17:22–31; Rom. 5:17; 8:19; 1 Cor. 15:24–28; Col. 1:13; Heb. 11:10,16; 12:28; 1 Pet. 2:4–10; 4:13; Rev. 1:6,9; 5:10; 11:15; 21—22

The Greek word rendered "kingdom" means kingship, royal power, royal rule. Thus it carries the idea of sovereignty. In an earthly sense it may refer to a territory ruled by a king. When used of God it connotes His kingly rule or sovereignty. The kingdom of God, therefore, refers to God's sovereign rule in both the natural and the spiritual universe, including the hearts of men who willfully submit to His rule. In chapter 7 it was noted that "the kingdom of God" and "the kingdom of heaven" are terms used by different writers in the new Testament to refer to the same thing. It was also noted that while the church is in the kingdom, it is not all of the kingdom.

Personal Learning Activity 12

Look up the phrase "kingdom of God/Heaven" in a Bible dictionary and the word "kingdom" in a regular dictionary. List the similarities and contrasts of God's kingdom and an earthly kingdom?

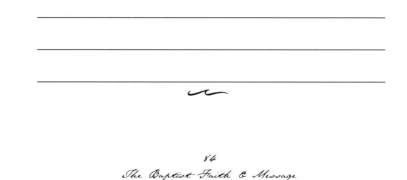

_____

_____

_____

The Kingdom as Sovereignty

Sovereignty here is used to denote God's rule in the universe and in the hearts of believers. As Creator, God has the right to be sovereign. While presenting this self-evident truth, the Bible also shows that Satan disputed this right, claiming sovereignty for himself (Luke 4:6–7). The incarnation of Christ was designed to prove Satan's claim to be false (1 John 3:8). This Jesus did through His death and resurrection.

That this is true may be seen in the examination of one Greek word rendered *power* *(exousia)*. This word means *out of being* or *power or authority exercised out of the nature of one's being*. When used of Satan it means tyrannical rule; when used of God it means benevolent rule.

The Nature of the Kingdom

When Jesus was examined by Pilate as to His kingship, He said, "My kingdom is not of [*ek*, out of] this world" (John 18:36). It is neither of a worldly nature nor to be established by worldly means. His is the kingdom of truth to which He came to witness (v. 37). "Truth" is related to salvation. Grace and truth are linked together. But in John's Gospel "grace" is not used after 1:17, while "truth" is used repeatedly throughout (twenty-five times in John). One may understand truth to include grace also.

So while God's sovereignty over the natural universe is presented in the New Testament, the major emphasis is placed upon God's reign in the hearts of all who receive Jesus Christ as Savior. Jesus sought to guard against the idea of an earthly territorial kingdom. "Neither shall they say, Lo here! or lo there! for, behold, the kingdom of God is within you" (Luke 17:21). But evidently the thought is that the kingdom of God is not an observable political unit; it is the reign of God among/within men. Some Baptists and others see Jesus at His return reigning on earth for a thousand years. One's position at this point is not a test of orthodoxy among Baptists.

So, in truth, the kingdom may be seen as having come when the King appeared; it is coming in the sense of being established in believers' hearts; it will come in final consummation at the Lord's return. Jesus taught that the kingdom is here. He taught His disciples to pray for the kingdom to come, and that at the end of the age the king will come in great power and glory.

The Christian and the Kingdom

As a citizen of God's kingdom, what is the Christian's part in its coming! Is he to establish the kingdom or to proclaim it? The New Testament teaches the latter. The Christian is to pray for the kingdom to come as God's will shall be done in earth as in heaven (Matt. 6:10). He is to seek the kingdom in that he proclaims it to lost men (Matt. 6:33). But the establishing of the kingdom

The Baptist Faith & Message

is the work of God in Christ through the Holy Spirit (1 Cor. 15:24–28).

Man is to receive the kingdom. Christians are to proclaim the kingdom. But only God brings the kingdom to its reality and final consummation.

SOME QUESTIONS FOR FURTHER THOUGHT

1. Are "kingdom of God" and "kingdom of heaven" the same or different?

2. What is the nature of God's kingdom?

3. What is the goal of history? Are there evidences even today that God is guiding events toward His ultimate redemptive purpose?

4. What is man's place with respect to the kingdom of God?

eleven

LAST THINGS

God, in His own time and in His own way, will bring the world to its appropriate end. According to His promise, Jesus Christ will return personally and visibly in glory to the earth; the dead will be raised; and Christ will judge all men in righteousness. The unrighteous will be consigned to hell, the place of everlasting punishment. The righteous in their resurrected and glorified bodies will receive their reward and will dwell forever in heaven with the Lord.

Isa. 2:4; 11:9; Matt. 16:27; 18:8-9; 19:28; 24:27,30,36,44; 25:31–46; 26:64; Mark 8:38; 9:43–48; Luke 12:40,48; 16:19–26; 17:22–37; 21:27–28; John 14:1–3; Acts 1:11; 17:31; Rom. 14:10; 1 Cor. 4:5; 15:24–28,35–58; 2 Cor. 5:10; Phil. 3:20–21; Col. 1:5; 3:4; 1 Thess. 4:14–18; 5:1 ff.; 2 Thess. 1:7 ff.; 2; 1 Tim. 6:14; 2 Tim. 4:1,8; Titus 2:13; Heb. 9:27–28; James 5:8; 2 Pet. 3:7 ff.; 1 John 2:28; 3:2; Jude 14; Rev. 1:18; 3:11; 20:1 to 22:13

"Eschatology" means the science of last things. Unfortunately this definition focuses upon the end of the age, when actually eschatology carries a broader meaning. It points to the end or goal of history. But it also means that God is active in history, directing it toward that goal.

Men speak of realized eschatology and unrealized eschatology. The former means that God's kingdom has already come. In the incarnation of Christ, God broke into the natural historical process to effect its goal according to His redemptive will. The latter points to the consummation of that will, when Christ shall come in full redemption of the saved and judgment for the lost. It is in this dual sense that one may understand Christ's presence now and His promised return. New Testament writers speak of living in the "last days." One must not think of this only in terms of man's calendar. It must be seen in the light of God's purpose. The "last days" may refer to the end of time or may be regarded as encompassing the period from Jesus' resurrection and ascension to His visible return in glory. With these things in mind certain things should be considered as to the Lord's return and the end of the age.

The Teachings of Jesus

That Jesus taught His return at the end of the age is quite clear (Matt. 16:27; John 5:28–29; 14:2). Matthew 16:28 is subject to dispute as to its meaning. "There may be some standing here, which shall not taste death, till they see the Son of man coming in his kingdom." Some take it literally and say that Jesus was mistaken as to the time element. However, in Jewish thought any significant event in history was regarded as God coming into history. With this in mind, others relate it to Jesus' transfiguration, resurrection, or the destruction of Jerusalem in A.D. 70. But all of the twelve lived beyond the first of these events and all but Judas beyond the second. Only some lived beyond the third. It would seem that this event satisfies Jesus' words. For with the fall of Jerusalem, Christianity was considered as separate from Judaism. Thus liberated, it was able to move out with even greater power.

Jesus' most extended teaching about the end of the age is found in Matthew 24—25. (See Mark 13; Luke 21:5–36.) These passages deal with these events: the destruction of Jerusalem, the Lord's return, and the end of the age.

Jesus warned against false signs of His return (Matt. 24:4–7). He said that when He comes all will see Him (24:23–31). His coming is certain even as the fall of Jerusalem is certain (24:32–35). But the time itself is hidden in the mind of the Father (24:36; Mark 13:32; Acts 1:7). Note that Jesus said that not even He knew the time (v. 36). In His humanity He accepted the limitations of such. He spoke only what the Father told Him (John 5:30; 7:16; 8:26). And the Father had not spoken this to Him. If Jesus did not know the date, it is futile for men to try to determine it. Jesus said that life would go on its normal way—and then would come the end (Matt. 24:37–41). Thus the return of the Lord is always imminent. For that reason believers should be alert and busy for the Lord at all times (24:42–46). In Matthew 25, Jesus gave parables relating to the end of the age.

Jesus never spoke of His return in terms of time but of condition— "When the Son of man shall come in his glory" (Matt. 25:31). "When" (hoten) refers to condition, not time. When the condition is right, that is the time. (See also Matt. 24:15,32–33; 26:29.) When the condition is right in God's judgment, that will be the time of the Lord's return. The most definite word of Jesus about the time of His coming is in Matthew 24:14. "And this gospel of the kingdom shall be preached in all the world for a witness unto all nations; and then shall the end come." But even here the time is governed by the condition. Christians should be busy creating the condition, and leave the time with God (Acts 1:7–8).

So Jesus taught that His return is certain and imminent; it will be sudden and universal; His people are to be alert and busy creating the condition in men's hearts; and only the Father knows the time. When He returns there will be the resurrection which will be followed by judgment and salvation, depending upon one's relation to Him. Jesus was explicit in His teachings about His second coming.

Read Matthew 24–25; Mark 13; and Luke 21:5–36. From these teachings by Jesus on last things, make a list of specific things He said about the end of the age.

The Blessed Hope of Believers

Paul wrote to Titus that Christians should live "righteously, and godly, in this present world; looking for that blessed hope, and the glorious appearing of the great God and our Saviour Jesus Christ" (Titus 2:12–13). That this "blessed hope" was real to first-century Christians is evident from Acts through Revelation. The author of Hebrews looked back in faith to Jesus' first coming and forward in assurance to His second coming (Heb. 9:28). Scoffers, judging by man's calendar, began to doubt the Lord's return. But Peter assured that it was certain by God's timetable, and on that basis urged holy living (2 Pet. 3).

So certain were the early Christians as to the imminency of the Lord's return that they thought in terms of their own lifetime. Rather than being in error, as some skeptics hold, they were doing exactly as Jesus had said. Paul spoke in terms of "we" (1 Cor. 15:51). Some generation would be alive when Jesus returned. And his was the only living one at the time. When it happened it would be "in a moment" (v. 52). In a time so small that it cannot be divided, Jesus will appear. It will be "in the twinkling of an eye" or in the buzzing of a gnat's wing. So quickly! At that time "the dead shall be raised incorruptible, and we shall be changed" (v. 52). Note "we" again.

The Thessalonian Christians were concerned lest they should be taken to be with the Lord at His return, leaving their dead, believing loved ones behind (1 Thess. 4:13–18). Paul assured them that at that event "the dead in Christ shall rise first" or before the living shall be taken (v. 16). "Then we [note "we" again] which are alive and remain shall be caught up together with them in the clouds, to meet the Lord in the air: and so shall we ever be with the Lord" (v. 17).

No doubt whatsoever! And this should be the blessed hope of all believers.

Personal Learning Activity 14

Why should the return of Jesus be considered the blessed hope of believers?

_____

_____

_____

_____

_____

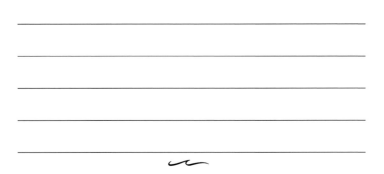

Problems Concerning Last Things

Since the New Testament speaks in broad terms about last things, it is to be expected that problems would arise as to the interpretation of details. For instance, interpreters differ as to the number of comings, resurrections, judgments, and the millennium, along with certain other details as to the end of the age. It is not the province of this work to deal with these differences. It is sufficient to say that one's position as to details has never been a test of orthodoxy among Baptists.

Baptists believe that Jesus is coming again. The dead shall be raised. Following judgment, the saved shall be forever with the Lord in glory and the lost forever with the devil in hell (Rev. 20:10 to 22:5). One's destiny in heaven or hell will not be determined at the judgment. It will only reveal the state in which one abode at death or the state in which the living abide when the Lord returns. That state will be eternal. The judgment will determine degrees of reward in heaven or punishment in hell.

In the meantime "the Spirit and the bride say, Come. And let him that heareth say, Come. And let him that is athirst come. And whosoever will [is willing], let him take the water of life freely" (Rev. 22:17).

The Lord says, "Surely I come quickly." And those who share the blessed hope say, "Amen. Even so, come, Lord Jesus" (Rev. 22:20).

The author wrote, "One's destiny in heaven or hell will not be determined at the judgment. It will only reveal the state in which one abode at death or the state in which the living abide when the Lord returns." What do you believe this statement means?

_____

_____

_____

_____

_____

The author wrote, "The judgment will determine degrees of reward in heaven or punishment in hell." Do you believe this statement is true? Explain your answer.

_____

_____

_____

_____

_____

SOME QUESTIONS FOR FURTHER THOUGHT

1. What is the distinction between realized and unrealized eschatology?

2. What are the signs against which Jesus warned as to the end of the age?

3. What does the word imminency mean with respect to Jesus' return? Distinguish between condition and time in this regard.

4. Should Jesus return today, what would He find you doing?

PRACTICES
OF THE FAITH

EVANGELISM AND MISSIONS

EDUCATION

STEWARDSHIP

COOPERATION

twelve

EVANGELISM AND MISSIONS

*It is the duty and privilege of every follower of Christ and of every church of
the Lord Jesus Christ to endeavor to make disciples of all nations. The new
birth of man's spirit by God's Holy Spirit means the birth of love for others.
Missionary effort on the part of all rests thus upon a spiritual necessity of the
regenerate life, and is expressly and repeatedly commanded in the teachings
of Christ. It is the duty of every child of God to seek constantly to win the
lost to Christ by personal effort and by all other methods in harmony with
the gospel of Christ.*

Gen. 12:1–3; Ex. 19:5–6; Isa. 6:1–8; Matt. 9:37–38; 10:5–15;
13:18–30,37–43; 16:19; 22:9–10; 24:14; 28:18–20; Luke 10:1–18;
24:46–53; John 14:11–12; 15:7–8,16; 17:15; 20:21; Acts 1:8; 2;
8:26–40; 10:42–48; 13:2–3; Rom. 10:13–15; Eph. 3:1–11; 1 Thess.
1:8; 2 Tim. 4:5; Heb. 2:1–3; 11:39 to 12:2; 1 Pet. 2:4–10; Rev. 22:17

In simplest terms, evangelism and missions involve sharing what one has
received. Persons become Christians by receiving the gospel in the fullest
sense of the word. Those receiving it fulfill their roles as Christians by sharing the good news with others. So it is both a privilege and an obligation.
When persons receive a new nature through regeneration by the Holy Spirit
they have a love for others, which should lead them to want others to have a
similar experience.

Missions and evangelism find their ultimate source in the heart of God.
Matthew 28:7 is highly suggestive. God sent an angel to roll away the stone
from the empty tomb and to tell the women that Jesus had risen. Then he
said, "And go quickly, and tell his disciples that he is risen from the dead;
and, behold, he goeth before you into Galilee; there shall ye see him: *lo, I
have told you*" (author's italics). These italicized words were the last ones
recorded as spoken by the angel. He had fulfilled his mission. From that time
on the responsibility to tell the good news rested upon those who had heard
it.

It has been and always will be this way. Those who have received the gospel
are to share it. This obligation God placed upon redeemed people, not upon
angels. If believers do not tell the story, it will not be told.

Commissioned to Share

Following His resurrection Jesus gave various missionary commissions to His disciples (Matt. 28:18–20; Luke 24:46–49; John 20:21–23; Acts 1:8). An analysis of Matthew 28:18–20 is most revealing. This Great Commission was given by the risen Christ. His redemptive work was finished. Its propagation must be done by His people, with His abiding presence through His Spirit.

Jesus did not command them to "go." Not for one moment did Jesus entertain the idea that they would *not* go. The only command was to "make disciples." This involved leading people to become Jesus' disciples or to receive Him as Lord and Savior. Having done so they were to baptize and teach (participles) them to observe all that He had commanded.

Personal Learning Activity 16

Write the words "make disciples" on the first line below. Using key words like ministry, worship, study, train, and others, list the most important actions involved in making disciples. What Scripture passages give guidance in how to make disciples? Also, list ways to make practical what is said in these verses.

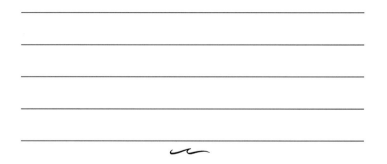

Those to whom Jesus spoke these words were the apostles plus others. "Some doubted" (v. 17) probably means others who had not previously seen Jesus alive after His resurrection. This commission was given not to a select few but to all who follow Jesus. The commission was given to the church (Eph. 3:9–11). It is every Christian's job.

Life of the Church

Missions/evangelism is the life of the church. This is true numerically, even for Baptists, who do not practice infant baptism and who avoid catechisms and similar methods of reaching people. Even more important, the souls of people everywhere depend upon it.

One may even say that the soul of the church itself depends upon it. History records that the church in Jerusalem refused to accept the challenge of missions, whereas the one in Antioch did accept it (Acts 13:1). Thus the

The Baptist Faith & Message

center of spiritual power shifted from the one to the other. Church history records that the times of greatest spiritual death have been those periods when evangelism and missions were at their lowest ebb. Conversely the times of greatest spiritual power have been those when the tides of evangelism and missions have been at their highest level.

Baptist history in America speaks to this truth. In 1814 Baptists divided over the question of missions. The antimissionary/evangelism group has dwindled away almost to the point of nonexistence. The missionary group has flourished to become the largest evangelical group in America.

The future of Baptists is linked with their dedication and zeal in sharing the good news. George W. Truett once said that the church that is not missionary in spirit and practice does not deserve the ground upon which its building stands. For, quoted he, "The earth is the Lord's, and the fulness thereof; the world, and they that dwell therein" (Ps. 24:1).

What is true of a church is true of every Christian. For what each has received from the Lord he should share with others. Jesus never commanded His people to be successful, but to be faithful. They are to be faithful in sowing the seed and telling the story of salvation. The results are His.

SOME QUESTIONS FOR FURTHER THOUGHT

1. How are evangelism and missions related?

2. Why does God hold Christians and not angels responsible for preaching the gospel?

3. What ways are evangelism and missions the life of the church?

4. What are you doing about evangelism and missions?

thirteen

EDUCATION

The cause of education in the Kingdom of Christ is coordinate with the causes of missions and general benevolence, and should receive along with these the liberal support of the churches. An adequate system of Christian schools is necessary to a complete spiritual program for Christ's people.

In Christian education there should be a proper balance between academic freedom and academic responsibility. Freedom in any orderly relationship of human life is always limited and never absolute. The freedom of a teacher in a Christian school, college, or seminary is limited by the preeminence of Jesus Christ, by the authoritative nature of the Scriptures, and by the distinct purpose for which the school exists.

Deut. 4:1,5,9,14; 6:1–10; 31:12–13; Neh. 8:1–8; Job 28:28; Psalm 19:7 ff.; 119:11; Prov. 3:13 ff.; 4:1–10; 8:1–7,11; 15:14; Eccl. 7:19; Matt. 5:2; 7:24 ff.; 28:19–20; Luke 2:40; 1 Cor. 1:18–31; Eph. 4:11–16; Phil. 4:8; Col. 2:3,8–9; 1 Tim. 1:3–7; 2 Tim. 2:15; 3:14–17; Heb. 5:12 to 6:3; James 1:5; 3:17

"Education" is the process or result of leading one out of ignorance and incompleteness into knowledge and a well-rounded self. Neither "educate" nor "education" appears in the *King James Version* of the Scriptures. But such words as "edify," "instruct," and "teach" appear in abundance. Although Jesus is presented as having preached, He was never called a preacher. But He was repeatedly called "Teacher" or "Master" in the sense of a teacher or rabbi. A casual examination of the Gospels shows the emphasis that Jesus placed on teaching. His followers were called "disciples" or learners. And He told His people to make disciples and teach them (Matt. 28:20). Religious education is a vital part of the work in local Baptist churches. But education as used in this section refers primarily to Christian education through educational institutions of higher learning outside the local church.

Christian Education

Henry Ward Beecher said, "Education is the knowledge of how to use the whole of one's self." This is the goal of Christian education. It is education plus the Christian element, which is designed to give education of the highest order but which also enables one to live and understand life in terms of God's role in history as revealed in Jesus Christ.

Baptists believe that "the cause of education ... is coordinate with the causes of missions and general benevolence, and should receive along with these the liberal support of the churches. An adequate system of Christian schools is necessary to a complete spiritual program for Christ's people."

Southern Baptists are committed to the cause of Christian education. Except in the newest "pioneer" areas, most state conventions have one or more colleges and/or universities. The Southern Baptist Convention itself owns and operates six theological seminaries. Christian education is a vital part of its foreign mission work. The Education Commission of the Southern Baptist Convention is dedicated to improving and promoting ever higher standards in this field.

While far more Baptist students attend state schools of higher education, it is the conviction of the various Baptist bodies that the opportunity for Christian education should be provided for all who desire it.

Benefits from Christian Education

These benefits are evident among a trained ministry and training in other vocations which in turn provide stronger leadership in the churches and in the denomination.

According to Rufus W. Weaver, "The early Baptist ministers (in the South) were men of spiritual fervor, native ability, but possessing little education. In 1791 there was not a single college man in all the Baptist ministry of the South."[1] These are strange-sounding words in the present day when many pastors of rural churches have both college and seminary degrees.

Many of the brightest chapters in early Baptist history were written by men with no college education. But the broad scope of Baptist influence and effectiveness has been elevated through an educated ministry and other leadership in churches and in the denomination.

Someone said that education without religion will fill the world with clever devils. This is not to say that every person who does not attend a Christian college is a devil. Through the work of the church in the child's formative years, plus the church and the Baptist Student Unions in university centers, many of the most effective Baptist leaders come out of state schools.

But it would be a sad day for Baptists if their Christian schools ceased to exist. Their missionary ranks would be sadly depleted. The Christian emphasis would be lost in the training of many to whom the churches must look for leadership. And Baptists would be neglecting one of the most vital phases of their Christian responsibility.

Problems in Christian Education

Any worthwhile endeavor will encounter problems. Christian education is no exception. These problems involve such matters as the relation between the denomination and churches and the school; the relation of the administration (trustees and school executives) to the faculty, student body, alumni, college community, and society as a whole; finances; curriculum; and teaching methods.

In recent years Southern Baptists conducted a two-year study of such problems. It was concluded that the primary need was for a clearly stated philosophy of Christian education and a proper understanding between the school and the denomination as to the relationships and responsibilities of each. The denomination should be led to understand the function of a Christian institution of higher learning in its pursuit of and the teaching of truth. The college community should comprehend its role in relation to the churches, the denomination, and their leadership.

Finances comprise one of the most acute problems. It is impossible for any private school without a large endowment to compete on even terms with tax-supported schools. It was concluded by the study group that each Christian school should determine where to place its peculiar emphasis, and to develop in that area the highest type of education possible. No state convention should try to have more schools than it can afford. And Baptists should provide the funds necessary for a sound program of Christian education.

One of the most demanding problems hinges upon academic freedom and academic responsibility. This problem is not peculiar to Christian schools. However, due to their nature as Christian institutions the problem is compounded.

In a Christian school, academic freedom and academic responsibility must be in balance. The school and its sponsoring body should endeavor to protect academic freedom. The faculty member should exercise academic responsibility. Should there be a violation of this freedom/responsibility, it is hardly possible that the problem can be handled in the public forum of a state or national convention. It should be treated by the elected trustees and administration of the institution, both of which should be sensitive to the rights of the teacher and to the general doctrinal position of the denomination.

When a professor accepts a teaching position in any school, he or she thereby accepts a limitation of personal freedom and the responsibility of teaching within the framework of the general beliefs of the sponsoring body. "The freedom of a teacher in a Christian school, college, or seminary is limited by the pre-eminence of Jesus Christ, by the authoritative nature of the Scriptures, and by the distinct purpose for which the school exists." No one should propose to teach in such a school who cannot in good conscience accept this limitation.

The Southern Baptist Convention as such has never required seminary teachers to sign any given statement of faith. The seminaries themselves do make such a requirement. Some have drawn up their own statements of prin-

ciples; some use "The Baptist Faith and Message" for this purpose.

Baptists believe in Christian education. They should provide it, pray for it, encourage it, and finance it so that it may fulfill its place in the work of Christ.

SOME QUESTIONS FOR FURTHER THOUGHT

1. Do you agree or disagree that the primary need in Christian education is a well-defined philosophy of Christian education?

2 Should problems rising out of Christian education be handled by the administration and trustees of schools or by the annual Convention? What does the denomination owe to its schools? What do the schools owe to the denomination?

3. Should there be a balance between academic freedom and academic responsibility? Who is responsible for maintaining that balance?

4. Should Baptists accept tax money to support their schools? If not, where can they look for financial support?

fourteen

STEWARDSHIP

God is the source of all blessings, temporal and spiritual; all that we have and are we owe to Him. Christians have a spiritual debtorship to the whole world, a holy trusteeship in the gospel, and a binding stewardship in their possessions. They are therefore under obligation to serve Him with their time, talents, and material possessions; and should recognize all these as entrusted to them to use for the glory of God and for helping others. According to the Scriptures, Christians should contribute of their means cheerfully, regularly, systematically, proportionately, and liberally for the advancement of the Redeemer's cause on earth.

Gen. 14:20; Lev. 27:30–32; Deut. 8:18; Mal. 3:8–12; Matt. 6:1–4,19–21; 19:21; 23:23; 25:14–29; Luke 12:16–21,42; 16:1–13; Acts 2:44–47; 5:1–11; 17:24–25; 20:35; rom. 6:6–22; 12:1–2; 1 Cor. 4:1–2; 6:19–20; 12; 16:1–4; 2 Cor. 8–9; 12:15; Phil. 4:10–19; 1 Pet. 1:18–19

In the Bible a steward was someone who was responsible for something which belonged to another (Gen. 15:2; 43:19; 44:4; Matt. 20:8). He was usually a slave placed over other slaves and over his owner's property (Luke 16:1). Paul referred to himself, Apollos, and Peter as stewards of the mysteries of God (1 Cor. 4:1–2). In this sense the pastor (bishop) is a steward of God (Titus 1:7). All Christians are to be "good stewards of the manifold grace of God" (1 Pet. 4:10).

Stewardship and Responsibility

Someone has defined stewardship as the acceptance from God of personal responsibility for all of life and life's affairs. This agrees with the Scriptures which teach that man is a steward of everything in his life: time, talents, and material possessions. A proper stewardship recognizes that God is the source of all blessings, that He both gives and owns them, and that man is a steward of them to use them for man's good and God's glory.

In discussing stewardship Paul asked, "What hast thou that thou didst not receive?" (1 Cor. 4:7). So whatever material, personal, or spiritual possessions a Christian has, they should not be a reason for self-glory but a means by which to give glory to God. To be sure, a proper use of possessions will be rewarded by God, even as an abuse of them brings God's judgment (Matt. 25:14–30; 24:45–51). These passages suggest that a faithful stewardship is evidence that one is a Christian, and that an abuse of stewardship indicates that one is not a Christian. It is a matter for sober contemplation (see Luke 16:1–14).

With respect to the stewardship of the gospel Paul said, "I am debtor" (Rom. 1:14). He was not in debt to other men because of what he had received from them, but because of what he had received from God. He was under obligation to share it with all men.

This obligation rests upon every Christian. A believer is to share the gospel through personal witnessing as well as by personal example. Jesus told His followers to witness; He also told them to be a witness. One's very life should testify to the saving power of Jesus Christ. And a believer should give of material possessions to enable others to preach and teach the gospel where he or she personally cannot go.

Stewardship of Possessions

One of Jesus' greatest emphases was upon people and their material possessions. Knowing the selfish nature of people, Christ sought to free them from the tyranny of things, and to lead them to use things for helping others both physically and spiritually. A large portion of the Sermon on the Mount dealt with the Christian and money (Matt. 6:19–34).

Rather than to amass treasures on earth, believers are to accumulate them in heaven (vv. 19–21). How can they lay up treasures in heaven? By investing their resources—time, talent, and money in people who may go or are going to heaven. The Christian should not have double vision, with one eye fastened on heaven and the other fastened on things of earth.

"No man can serve [be a slave to] two masters [owners]: for either he will hate the one, and love the other; or else he will hold to the one, and despise the other. Ye cannot serve [be a slave to] God and mammon" (v. 24). Both owners demand absolute loyalty and service; one person cannot give both to two people. Obviously the Christian is to be a slave to God. Christians cannot serve God and mammon, but they can serve God through mammon.

Christians should not be overly anxious about material things. Rather they will trust God for necessities and be concerned wholly with serving God (vv. 25–32). Their primary concern will be to use all of life to introduce others to the kingly rule of God (v. 33).

Jesus knew the vicious nature of things when not used for God's glory. This is the message in the parable of the rich fool (Luke 12:16–21). It was given in response to a dispute between two brothers over their inheritance (vv. 13–15). He warned both to guard against covetousness or the desire for more things. His conclusion is stated in verse 20. "Thou fool, this night thy soul shall be required of thee [these things are requiring thy soul of thee]: then whose shall those things be, which thou hast provided?" The rich young ruler

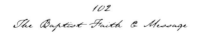

was foolish for two reasons. He thought that he possessed things when all the while they possessed him. And instead of using them to serve God and man, he was amassing them to be fought over by his survivors. The event of the rich young ruler is also a classic example of how one's love for and trust in money can keep one from God (Luke 18:18–25).

The point in the parable of the unjust or shrewd steward is that while one has his stewardship he should use it in such a way that when he gets to heaven he will be welcomed by those who precede him as the result of his proper use of his stewardship (Luke 16:1–9). It is thus that the Christian can lay up treasures in heaven.

The Measure of Stewardship

The truth that all belongs to God means that all should be used for His glory. Even that which the Christian spends for personal needs should serve God. But what portion should be given for direct support of God's work in the world?

The Old Testament clearly taught the giving of the tithe or one tenth of the increase. Actually the Mosaic law includes three tithes (Lev. 27:30–33; Num. 29:39; Deut. 12:5–6). The first tithe was to support the levites and the tabernacle. The second tithe was to provide food to be eaten before the Lord. The third tithe, given every three years, was for charity. Malachi 3:8 speaks of "tithes and offerings," probably the first tithe plus offerings.

There is some question as to whether or not the tithe is binding upon the Christian, since it is a part of the Mosaic law. It should be noted, however, that the tithe antedates that code (Gen. 14:18–20; 28:22). Furthermore, Jesus never lowered an Old Testament standard. He lifted each from the letter to the spirit (Matt. 5:20–48). He commended the Pharisees for tithing, but condemned their lack of mercy (Matt. 23:23).

No mention is made of Jesus' tithing. But certainly Joseph, who was "just" (one who lived strictly by the law), did. In all likelihood he taught Jesus to do so. As a Jew, Jesus never broke one of the Mosaic laws. Tithing was a pet doctrine among the Pharisees. They criticized Jesus for ignoring their rules of conduct. But no record shows criticism of him for not tithing. Much of this is inductive reasoning and argument from silence, but it is highly suggestive.

However, having said this, it is clear that Jesus taught that God owns all, man is but a steward, and that all things should be used for God's glory. He did not count or weigh the gift, but measured the love behind it. In the event of the widow's mite (about one fifth of a cent), Jesus made no comment about the large gifts of the rich. He said that the widow had given more than all of them (Mark 12:41–44). She gave "all her living" and probably went hungry that night because of it.

The Lord measures the gift by the love and sacrifice it involves. He does not look simply at what one has before the gift is made but at what is left after it is given. Christians should not claim to have given the widow's mite until they have given all that they have. Truly, "It is more blessed to give than to receive" (Acts 20:35).

Paul's words to the Corinthian church present a pattern in Christian giving (1 Cor. 16:2). "Upon the first day of the week [day for Christian worship] let every one of you lay by him in store, as God hath prospered him, that there be no gatherings when I come." Note the period, persons, place, proportion, provision, and purpose of the collection. Verses 3–4 give the plan for the protection of the collection. There is also a stewardship in administering the Lord's money.

Some note that here Paul made no mention of the tithe. Such would have been given for the normal support of the Lord's work. The issue here is offerings given as a special gift for Palestinian relief. But the principles given here may apply to all Christian giving.

"According to the Scriptures, Christians should contribute of their means cheerfully, regularly, systematically, proportionately, and liberally for the advancement of the Redeemer's cause on earth."

Personal Learning Activity 17

Secure a monthly budget report from your church. Examine the amounts and ways money is spent for the Lord's work. On the lines below make notes concerning any questions you have. Then on a separate piece of paper, write a letter of appreciation to the finance committee for its wise stewardship.

_____

_____

_____

_____

SOME QUESTIONS FOR FURTHER THOUGHT

1. What is the scope of stewardship in the Bible? List some items or areas of which you are a steward.

2. In what sense are you a Christian debtor to other men? Is it because of what you receive from them or from God?

3. Should tithing be the goal or the starting point in Christian stewardship of possessions?

COOPERATION

Christ's people should, as occasion requires, organize such associations and conventions as may best secure cooperation for the great objects of the Kingdom of God. Such organizations have no authority over one another or over the churches. They are voluntary and advisory bodies designed to elicit, combine, and direct the energies of our people in the most effective manner. Members of New Testament churches should cooperate with one another in carrying forward the missionary, educational, and benevolent ministries for the extension of Christ's Kingdom. Christian unity in the New Testament sense is spiritual harmony and voluntary cooperation for common ends by various groups of Christ's people. Cooperation is desirable between the various Christian denominations, when the end to be attained is itself justified, and when such cooperation involves no violation of conscience or compromise of loyalty to Christ and His Word as revealed in the New Testament.

Ex. 17:12; 18:17 ff.; Judg. 7:21; Ezra 1:3–4; 2:68–69; 5:14–15; Neh. 4; 8:1–5; Matt. 10:5–15; 20:1–16; 22:1–10; 28:19–20; Mark 2:3; Luke 10:1 ff.; Acts 1:13–14; 2:1 ff; 4:31–37; 13:2–3; 15:1–35; 1 Cor. 1:10–17; 3:5–15; 12; 2 Cor. 8–9; Gal. 1:6–10; Eph. 4:1–16; Phil. 1:15–18

Baptists are an independent but a cooperating people. The term "Cooperative Program" testifies to the latter fact. It is the term used by Southern Baptists to denote their program of giving for the support of Christ's work throughout the earth. It is a cooperation freely and independently given. Such a cooperative effort protects the autonomy of each group, and at the same time harnesses the spiritual energies and material resources of Southern Baptists for the purpose of directing the energies of the denomination for the spreading of the gospel.

Scriptural Grounds for Cooperation

Though Baptists, due to the independent nature of local churches, were slow in organizing even district associations, there are scriptural grounds for cooperative endeavor in matters of mutual interest. The first such effort was with regard to doctrinal purity. This is seen in the Jerusalem conference held in A.D. 49 (Acts 15; Gal. 2). Representatives of the churches in Jerusalem and Antioch met to confer about the Judaizer controversy. This was a voluntary conference which carefully safeguarded the position of both churches. But the results gave a unity of support to a gospel of salvation by grace through faith as opposed to a message of works plus faith.

Another such cooperative effort is seen in Paul's rallying the churches of Macedonia and Greece to make an offering for the relief of suffering Jewish Christians in Palestine (1 Cor. 16:1; 2 Cor. 8–9). However, a study of the Corinthian passages shows that this was a voluntary effort in cooperation.

These are but two examples. But they are sufficient grounds upon which a cooperative work may be based.

History of Baptist Cooperation

The first organized convention of Baptists in America grew out of foreign missionary needs. The Baptist Society for the Propagation of the Gospel in Foreign Parts was organized in Philadelphia in 1812. This resulted in the founding of the Baptist General Convention, including all the Baptists in the United States. Meeting every three years, it was called the Triennial Convention. This convention was supported by individuals rather than by churches as such. As the convention expanded its interests beyond foreign missions, the churches became suspicious, fearing that it pointed toward a centralized Baptist authority. Finally the slavery issue became involved, and it was voted that no slaveholder could be appointed as a missionary. The members of the Southern states withdrew, and the Triennial Convention as such came to an end.

However, the convention's work did not cease. Societies were organized to carry on various phases of the work. Eventually this group formed what today is known as the American Baptist Convention. Many other conventions comprised of various ethnic groups have come into being through the years.

The Southern Baptist Convention was organized in Augusta, Georgia, in 1845. Today it is the largest of the Baptist groups, with a membership in cooperating churches of approximately fifteen million people. Actually, the Convention is composed of messengers from the cooperating churches who meet annually. Through its various agencies it carries on a continuing ministry both in the United States and in many other countries throughout the world.

Southern Baptist life is made possible through the voluntary cooperation of churches, district associations, state conventions, and the Southern Baptist Convention. Cooperating churches are found in every state in the United States. And yet each unit from the local church to the national Convention is separate and independent of all other units. It is a marvel of voluntary cooperation.

A pastor in another convention asked the writer the secret of the efficient, cooperative work among Southern Baptists. He wanted to know what pressure was applied to achieve this. The writer told him that there was no pres-

sure. There was only a sense of need for independent cooperation under the lordship of Christ in order to do the best work possible in carrying out God's redemptive purpose in the world. Through the Baptist World Alliance, Baptists around the world cooperate in a fellowship of love, prayer, and mutual concern in meeting the needs of men in the name and spirit of Christ.

This is the unity for which Baptists believe that Jesus prayed (John 17:21). "Christian unity in the New Testament sense is spiritual harmony and voluntary cooperation for common ends by various groups of Christ's people."

Personal Learning Activity 18

Complete the following statements about Southern Baptists:

1. The Southern Baptist Convention was organized in the city of_____ _____ in ____.

2. Today the Southern Baptist Convention is the _____ of all Baptist bodies.

3. Southern Baptist life is made possible through the _____ cooperation of _____, district _____, state _____, and the _____ _____ _____.

4. Southern Baptists carry on a wide range of ministries in the United States and around the world through the various _____ of the Convention.

5. Baptist around the world cooperate in a fellowship of love, prayer, and mutual concern for ministry in the name of Christ through the _____ _____ _____.

6. "Christian unity in the New Testament sense is spiritual _____ and voluntary _____ for common ends by various groups of God's people."

Unity, Not Union

In some quarters Southern Baptists have been called "the problem child" of American Protestantism. This is due to their refusal to become involved in various ecumenical movements whose stated ultimate goals are organic union of all church groups.

Various reasons have prompted Southern Baptists to avoid such movements. The overriding reason is that of ecclesiology. For instance, the National Council of Churches accepts only denominational bodies as members. The Southern Baptist Convention has no authority to commit the churches. Even should Southern Baptists want to join, they could not do so, being prevented by both themselves and the National Council of Churches.

But Southern Baptists do believe in cooperation with other denominations in matters of mutual interest which do not compromise their faith and practice as they understand the teachings of the New Testament. Such cooperation must involve "no violation of conscience or compromise of loyalty to Christ and His Word as revealed in the New Testament."

Baptists believe that Jesus prayed for spiritual unity and not for organic union. "That they all may be one; as thou, Father, art in me, and I in thee, that they also may be one in us" (John 17:21). "One" in the last phrase is not in the best manuscripts.

Father and Son are one in essence but two in outward manifestation. But there is unity in spirit, nature, and purpose. Jesus prayed that this same unity would prevail among His people. He did not pray that His eleven disciples would become one huge man, but that as individual persons they would experience the unity of spirit and purpose as seen in the Father and the Son. It is "I in them, and thou in me" (John 17:23). It was thus through the Holy Spirit that the disciples would know the fellowship which would make them a unity, not a union, in spirit and purpose.

That Baptists do share a unity of spirit with all who truly believe in Christ is evidenced by the words of A. H. Strong spoken at the first Baptist World Congress in 1905. "It is surely our duty to confess everywhere and always that we are first Christians, and only secondly Baptists. The tie which binds us to Christ is more important in our eyes than that which binds us to those of the same faith and order. We live in hope that the Spirit of Christ in us, and in all other Christian bodies, may induce such growth of mind and heart that the sense of unity in Christ may not only overtop and hide the fences of division, but may ultimately do away with these fences altogether."[1] But note that this is to come through an inner unity and not a union imposed from without.

George W. Truett spoke in a similar vein at the Baptist World Congress in 1939. "We profoundly rejoice in our spiritual union with all who love the Lord Jesus Christ in sincerity and truth. We cherish them as brothers in the saving grace of Christ, and heirs with us of life and immortality. We love their fellowship, and maintain that the spiritual union of all true believers in Christ is now, and will ever be, a blessed reality. This spiritual union does not depend on organizations, or forms, or ritual. It is deeper, higher, broader, and more stable than any and all organizations. Baptists joyfully cherish all these believers in Christ, as their brothers in the common salvation, whether they be found in any Protestant communion, or in a Catholic communion, or in any other communion, or in no communion."[2]

SOME QUESTIONS FOR FURTHER THOUGHT

1. Should cooperation exist only within the local church fellowship, or should it extend to the relation between Baptist churches?

2. What is the relation between Baptist bodies: local church, district association, state and national conventions, Baptist World Alliance?

3. Should Baptist churches seek ways of cooperation with other Christian groups? If so, in what areas and on what basis? Make a list of areas in which such cooperation is possible.

4. Why have Southern Baptists never been in the National (and World) Council of Churches?

5. What is the difference between Christian unity and organic church union?

SOCIAL IMPLICATIONS OF THE FAITH

THE CHRISTIAN
AND THE SOCIAL ORDER

PEACE AND WAR

RELIGIOUS LIBERTY

sixteen

THE CHRISTIAN AND THE SOCIAL ORDER

Every Christian is under obligation to seek to make the will of Christ supreme in his own life and in human society. Means and methods used for the improvement of society and the establishment of righteousness among men can be truly and permanently helpful only when they are rooted in the regeneration of the individual by the saving grace of God in Christ Jesus. The Christian should oppose, in the spirit of Christ, every form of greed, selfishness, and vice. He should work to provide for the orphaned, the needy, the aged, the helpless, and the sick. Every Christian should seek to bring industry, government, and society as a whole under the sway of the principles of righteousness, truth, and brotherly love. In order to promote these ends Christians should be ready to work with all men of good will in any good cause, always being careful to act in the spirit of love without compromising their loyalty to Christ and His truth.

Ex. 20:3–17; Lev. 6:2–5; Deut. 10:12; 27:17; Ps. 101:5; Mic. 6:8; Zech. 8:16; Matt. 5:13–16,43–48; 22:36–40; 25:35; Mark 1:29–34; 2:3 ff; 10:21; Luke 4:18–21; 10:27–37; 20:25; John 15:12; 17:15; Rom. 12–14; 1 Cor. 5:9–10; 6:1–7; 7:20–24; 10:23 to 11:1; Gal. 3:26–28; Eph. 6:5–9; Col 3:12–17; 1 Thess. 3:12; Philem.; James 1:27; 2:8

Baptists generally do not believe in a social gospel or that the kingdom of God can be established simply through social reform of an individual or of society as a whole. But Baptists do believe in a spiritual gospel which has social implications. For this reason they hold that every Christian should seek "to make the will of Christ supreme in his own life and in human society." He should pray—and work—to the end that God's will shall be done on earth.

Personal Regeneration Basic

Since all social injustice is rooted in sin, efforts for improving the social order and establishing righteousness must begin in the regeneration of the individual person. Then such efforts may prove to be permanently helpful. Someone said that Jesus was revolutionary but not a revolutionist. His gospel was dynamic but not dynamite. He sought to change society in a responsible, constructive way but never in an irresponsible, destructive one.

Jesus began with the individual and worked out into society. Rather than picket the home of Zaccheus, He entered it and led him to become His disciple. Thus He changed a crooked chief publican into a philanthropic tax commissioner (Luke 19:1–10). Nicodemus was a model citizen. But Jesus told him that if he were to experience the kingdom of God he must be born of the Spirit (John 3:3–8). Jesus repeatedly refused to be a bread-military-political Messiah (Matt. 4:1–4,8–10; John 6:5–15,24–58). Rather He came to seek and to save that which was lost (Luke 19:10). Yet His teachings clearly show His purpose of developing His followers into Christians whose lives would help to transform the social order (Matt. 5:13; 7:24).

Jesus rejected all efforts to establish His kingdom by violence or by forced reform from without (Matt. 11:12). Rather He proposed to redeem men and then to send them into society to change it into God's will and way. Christians are not to be of the world, but in it, changing it according to the purposes of Christ (John 17:15–18).

The Christian and Society

Jesus taught that Christians should be both salt and light in the world. The very presence of Christians should be a judgment upon all that is corrupt and evil. Their influence should be felt as in the spirit of Christ they oppose every form of greed, selfishness, and vice.

Jesus was opposed to every form of man's inhumanity to man. He recognized the evil systems which violated the dignity of human personality (such as slavery). But He attacked them from within, seeking to change men's hearts so that redeemed men would live together in peace and love (Eph. 2:14–22). Paul, Jesus' greatest interpreter, followed the same pattern (Eph. 6:5–9; Philem.). It is the pattern which should be used by every Christian.

Positively, the Christian should provide for the needs of orphans and widows (Jas. 1:27), and for all who are needy, helpless, and ill (Matt. 25:34–40; Luke 10:25–37). He should endeavor to bring the whole of society to live according to the principles of righteousness, truth, and love. But he should do so as a Christian, not merely as a social crusader (Jas. 2; 1 John 4:7–21).

Christian Citizenship

The Christian, while a citizen of the kingdom of God, is also a citizen of some nation. He should be a good citizen of both (Matt. 22:21).

God has ordained the institution of government. Therefore, every soul should be subject unto governmental rule (Rom. 13:1). One may not always agree with a given law. But so long as it does not violate the Christian's relation to God, the Christian should obey it (vv. 2–4). Through due process he may try to change such laws. But so long as it is the law, the Christian should obey it, not out of fear of punishment but out of a Christian conscience (v. 5). Even if he suffers under law it should be for his faith, not as a criminal (1 Pet. 4:15–16).

Through the centuries Christians have lived under all types of governments. They have suffered under many and been blessed under others. But whatever may be the form of the state, Jesus' words abide. "Let your light so shine before men, that they may see your good works, and glorify your Father which is in heaven" (Matt. 5:16).

Social Cooperation

In order to make the greatest impact upon society, "Christians should be ready to work with all men of good will in any good cause, always being careful to act in the spirit of love without compromising their loyalty to Christ and His truth."

Personal Learning Activity 19

Read the first part of the Sermon on the Mount (Matt. 5:1–9). Select two of the Beatitudes that speak of practical ways to better the lives of others. How can these truths be applied in your life? List some definite ways on the lines below.

_____

_____

_____

_____

To this end Baptists through the years have worked with other groups in meeting social problems of mutual concern (such as alcohol, narcotics, pornography, religious liberty, social ministries). One of the constant goals for Southern Baptists is to seek more and better ways of communicating and cooperating with other denominations at the local level in matters of common interest.

SOME QUESTIONS FOR FURTHER THOUGHT

1. What is the difference between a social gospel and a gospel which has social implications?

2. Should a Christian obey only those laws with which he agrees? When is a Christian justified in refusing to obey a law?

3. What are some positive ways by which a Christian can improve the social order?

4. On what basis should a Baptist work with other groups in social projects?

seventeen
PEACE AND WAR

It is the duty of Christians to seek peace with all men on principles of right-
eousness. In accordance with the spirit and teachings of Christ they should
do all in their power to put an end to war.
The true remedy for the war spirit is the gospel of our Lord. The supreme
need of the world is the acceptance of His teachings in all the affairs of men
and nations, and the practical application of His law of love.

Isa. 2:4; Matt. 5:9,38–48; 6:33; 26:52; Luke 22:36,38; Rom.
12:18–19; 13:1–7; 14:19; Heb. 12:14; Jas. 4:1–2

That peace is the desire of all right-thinking men is evident. Still, mankind
is constantly faced with war or the threat of it. Two historians have noted in
recent years that "in the last 3,421 years of recorded history only 268 have
seen no war."[1] Men talk of just and lasting peace. Perhaps just, but not lasting. The Prince of Peace Himself said that "wars and rumours of wars" are a
part of life as men live it (Matt. 24:6). The Bible holds forth no hope of a lasting peace until Jesus reigns supreme in men's hearts and in His universe. This
is not to condone war, but to recognize it as a constant problem.

Prophecy or Condition?

The angels sang of "glory to God in the highest, and on earth peace, good will
toward men" (Luke 2:14). This reads as though it were a prophecy of peace
on earth. But the Greek text reads "upon earth peace in the sphere of men of
good will." Some read it as "men well-pleasing to God." Thus rather than
being a prophecy, it is the condition whereby there may be peace on earth.
There will be no peace on earth among men until there is glory to God in the
highest, as men through faith in His Son submit to His will.

"From whence come wars and fightings among you? come they not hence,
even of your lusts that war in your members? Ye lust, and have not: ye kill,
and desire to have, and cannot obtain: ye fight and war, yet ye have not,
because ye ask not. Ye ask, and receive not, because ye ask amiss, that ye may
consume it upon your lusts" (Jas. 4:1–3). Note the progress: to lust and to kill,
if necessary, to get.

War in the individual heart? Yes. In a church fellowship? Yes. In the social
order? Yes. But in the international social order also. As long as there are lusts
and sin in men's hearts, there will be war. A sad picture, to be sure. But the
Bible gives no other for this age.

Reconciliation of man to God must precede reconciliation of man to man. So the Christian's first line of attack upon war and first effort to establish peace on earth must be in the hearts of men.

Personal Learning Activity 20

What is the origin of war and fighting? A biblical answer is found in James 4:1–3. Read this passage carefully. After you have read the passage, write the answer in your own words in the space provided.

_____

_____

_____

_____

_____

_____

_____

Jesus and War

Was Jesus an extreme pacifist, a "peace at any price" person? Hardly so. He died rather than give in to evil. He did not die in battle resisting evil with a sword. But He did show that there are some values worth dying for. He gave His life that He might establish the grounds for peace between God and man and between man and man (2 Cor. 5:17–21; Eph. 2:13–17).

What about Jesus and the sword? "Put up again thy sword into his place: for all they that take the sword shall perish with the sword" (Matt. 26:52). Did Jesus mean that there is no place for the sword in the practical affairs of men and nations? To follow this line of reasoning to its end would mean total disarmament of nations set to resist evil and oppression, disbanding of all police forces, and refusal to protect even one's family and home. Such a procedure would turn the world into a jungle ruled by criminals and tyrants, and in which all moral and spiritual values would disappear from the social order.

In the upper room Jesus reminded the apostles that when He sent them on a preaching mission without either money or provisions, they had lacked nothing. "But now [by contrast], he that hath a purse, let him take it, and likewise his scrip; and he that hath no sword, let him sell his garment, and buy one" (Luke 22:36). Already Judas had gone for the authorities who would make the arrest. Soon Jesus would go to Gethsemane for a prayer rendezvous with God. He would die, but in a manner designed of God. He was not to be taken until He was ready. Seeing two swords, probably belonging to the owner of the house, the apostles pointed them out. Jesus said, "It is enough." Enough for what? They were not to storm the tower of Antonia in rebellion against Rome. They were to protect Jesus until He was ready to be arrested. In Gethsemane Peter had one sword. Where was the other? With the disciples near the entrance to the garden? Since the word "watch" (Matt. 26:38; Mark 14:34) may also mean "be on guard," did Jesus establish an outer and inner guard? Luke 22:49–50 suggests that the disciples had two swords. While some were asking if they should strike with the sword, Peter did so without waiting for an answer. He did what he understood that Jesus had told him. He was guarding Jesus. However, Jesus was now ready to be taken. Therefore, He told Peter to put up his sword or he would get himself killed for no reason.[2]

Some interpreters see Luke 22:36 as instructions for the apostles to take a sword when they went on missionary journeys outside Palestine or in enemy territory. This seems to take the verse entirely out of context. The reason for the sword is stated in verse 37, not in verse 35. But either interpretation means that on occasion Jesus did counsel use of the sword—but for defense, not offense.

From this one may deduce that while Jesus abhorred war, He did teach the right of defending one's person, home, and nation. The word "kill" in the Sixth Commandment means to commit murder (Matt. 19:18). It has no reference to killing in war, police action, or capital punishment.

Personal Learning Activity 21

Do you agree or disagree with the author's statement: "The word 'kill' in the sixth commandment means to commit murder. It has no reference to killing in war, police action, or capitol punishment." ____agree ___disagree.
Explain your response to this question.

_____

_____

_____

_____

_____

The Christian and War

Paul said, "If it be possible, as much as lieth in you, live peaceably with all men" (Rom. 12:18). Some people will not let others be at peace with them. But what goes out of the Christian should be conducive to peace. The cause of strife should not originate in the Christian's life.

This principle applies to both men and nations. It may not be possible to live in peace. But the Christian's resistance to evil should be out of love for the good. Christians, like all sane men, should abhor war as such. But there is a difference between offensive war for greed and defensive war to preserve that which is good.

The United States Government grants exemption from combat to persons who meet their qualifications as conscientious objectors. But otherwise, as a Christian citizen of a state, good citizenship requires one to defend his nation if it is threatened by aggression. One should not accept peace at any price if it means the loss of those elements which make for righteousness.

Jesus' words in Matthew 5:38–41 have to do with the Christian's personal relationships. The principle is the opposite of the law of retaliation, "an eye for an eye, and a tooth for a tooth." "Resist not evil" means that one should not resist the evil person with a like evil. To turn the other cheek means that one should go the limit in trying to preserve peace. But when smitten by the Temple police, Jesus did not actually turn His other cheek (John 18:23). Rather He remonstrated against the smiters. The words agree with Paul's words in Romans 12:18. The Christian should do all that he can to prevent strife. Its cause should not come from him. But self-defense is another matter, and especially defense of others and of principles of righteousness and truth.

Mullins has a fine comment on the warlike spirit. "The gospel is clearly opposed to the warlike spirit when that spirit is based on any form of unrighteousness. It would be going too far to say that Christianity is inconsistent or incompatible with every form of war. There are forms of war and oppression which only war can destroy. But the desire for national greatness, based on the injury of other nations, is wholly alien to the spirit of Christianity. Christ died for the human race. And while national feeling and patriotic loyalty are not opposed to the gospel, yet every form of such feeling which forgets the rights of others is opposed to it. A narrow nationalism which forgets other nations is an antichristian ideal."[3] Such a statement is in keeping with the teachings of Jesus.

The Christian and Peace

Within himself, a Christian should be a person of peace. He should do all within his power to promote peace among men and nations. He should see in the gospel of Christ the true remedy for the war spirit.

Recognizing that men will not be at peace with themselves until they are at peace with God, Christian people should both live and preach the gospel among and to a world caught in the power of the evil one. Someone said that one missionary is a greater power in the cause of world peace than is a battleship.

The supreme need of the world is the acceptance of Christ and His teachings and the practical living of the law of Christian love among men. The Christian should endeavor to meet this need through personal example, witness, and the support of those who live and witness for Christ throughout the world.

SOME QUESTIONS FOR FURTHER THOUGHT

1. What is the New Testament basis for a just and lasting peace? Does the Bible promise such in this age? Where should one begin in seeking to establish peace among men?

2. Does the Bible disapprove of war as a way of life? Did Jesus teach that war is ever justified? If so, what kind of war?

3. What should be the Christian citizen's attitude toward a defensive war? How far should one go in turning the other cheek?

4. Does the Sixth Commandment forbid defensive warfare? What would be the ultimate result of extreme pacifism in a world society where many men and nations follow the war spirit?

eighteen
RELIGIOUS LIBERTY

God alone is Lord of the conscience, and He has left it free from the doctrines and commandments of men which are contrary to His Word or not contained in it. Church and state should be separate. The state owes to every church protection and full freedom in the pursuit of its spiritual ends. In providing for such freedom no ecclesiastical group or denomination should be favored by the state more than others. Civil government being ordained of God, it is the duty of Christians to render loyal obedience thereto in all things not contrary to the revealed will of God. The church should not resort to the civil power to carry on its work. The gospel of Christ contemplates spiritual means alone for the pursuit of its ends. The state has no right to impose penalties for religious opinions of any kind. The state has no right to impose taxes for the support of any form of religion. A free church in a free state is the Christian ideal, and this implies the right of free and unhindered access to God on the part of all men, and the right to form and propagate opinions in the sphere of religion without interference by the civil power. Gen. 1:27; 2:7; Matt. 6:6–7,24; 16:26; 22:21; John 8:36; Acts 4:19–20; Rom. 6:1–2; 13:1–7; Gal. 5:1,13; Phil. 3:20; 1 Tim. 2:1–2; Jas. 4:12; 1 Pet. 2:12–17; 3:11–17; 4:12–19

Religious liberty is the mother of all true freedom. It is rooted in the very nature of both God and man created in God's likeness (Gen. 1:27). It implies the competency of the soul in religion, and denies to any person, civil government, or religious system the right to come between God and man (1 Tim. 2:1–6).

Definition of Religious Liberty

Religious liberty is "a term denoting the right of every man to worship God as his conscience dictates. It means equality before the law, not only of all forms of the Christian faith, but also of other religions."[1] And one might add "of no religion." Man is free not to worship God if he chooses not to do so.

Religious liberty is not religious toleration. Religious toleration is a privilege granted by man. Religious liberty is a right bestowed by God. For liberty involves responsibility and demands inner and personal controls (Rom. 6:6–18; Gal. 5:13–16).

Find the two expressions "religious toleration" and "religious liberty" in an encyclopedia, history book, or contemporary magazine. Read the material and make notes on the differences in the space below. Express a prayer of gratitude to God for blessing our nation with a constitutional guarantee of religious liberty.

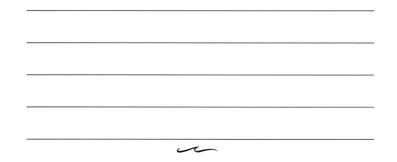

Scriptural Basis of Religious Liberty

Religious liberty does not rest upon a legal document of a political state. It is rooted in the Bible. Freedom is inherent in man's nature as God created him (Gen. 1:27). Even God does not coerce man against his will. He is responsible for his choices, but he is free to choose (Gen 3). This freedom-responsibility means that God alone is Lord of man's conscience. And God has ordained that man's conscience shall be "free from the doctrines and commandments of men which are contrary to His Word or not contained in it."

Thus religious liberty is rooted in the lordship of Christ. Therefore, when man's commandments conflict with God's will, the Christian should obey God and not man (Acts 4:18–20). When faced with the choice of saying, "Caesar is Lord" or "Jesus is Lord," the Christian should say the latter (Rom. 10:9, RSV). True liberty is found only in Christ (John 8:36; Rom. 8:1–2), and is to be exercised in the power and under the guidance of the Holy Spirit (Rom. 8:5–9; 2 Cor. 3:17). Christians should be good citizens of the state, but when its laws conflict with God's laws they should say, "We ought to obey God rather than men" (Acts 5:29).

Separation of Church and State

Mullins' fifth axiom of religion is "The religio-civic axiom: A free Church in a free State."[2] This axiom was clearly stated by Jesus. "Render therefore unto Caesar the things which are Caesar's; and unto God the things which are God's" (Matt. 22:21). A free state does not create religious liberty. It recognizes and respects it. But religious freedom is essential in making a free state.

Separation of church and state does not mean that they have no relations whatsoever. Jesus recognized the rights and functions of the state (Matt. 22:15–21). The early Christian missionaries used roads and sea lanes provided by the state, and at times claimed the state's protection (Acts 18:12–17; 21:27–39; 22:25–30; 25:10–12). Christians as citizens were told to submit to the authority of the state (Rom. 13:1–8; 1 Pet. 2:12–17).

Church and state are mutually related in the normal affairs of life. The state provides a favorable atmosphere in which the church can do its work (such as fire and police protection, national security, postal service, roads and streets, general social stability). And the churches, in turn, should produce through the gospel the type of Christian citizens which will contribute to a stable social order.

At the same time church and state are mutually exclusive. Neither should seek to control the other or to use it in filling its peculiar role. Neither should propose to tell the other how to discharge its responsibility. The church should not seek to use the state for its purposes. The state should not commandeer the church for political ends. The state should not favor one religion above another. It is the opinion of this writer that no taxes should be levied against property used strictly for religious purposes. The churches should not receive tax funds for use in discharging their educational, healing, or spiritual responsibility. The church should be free to determine its programs of worship, evangelism, and missionary activities. But such should be done within the legal structure of the social order designed for the good of all citizens.

Quite obviously there are gray areas in the relationship between church and state. These are subject to interpretation. But one thing is clear. Neither church nor state should exercise authority over the other. History records that a free church in a free state proves a blessing to both.

Personal Learning Activity 23

Carefully read each statement below and mark the true statements with a T and the false statements with an F.

1.__ Separation of church and state means that the two do not relate in any way.
2.__ The state should provide the kind of atmosphere in which the church can do its work, and the church should produce the kind of citizens that contribute to a stable social order.
3.__ Neither church nor state should seek to control or use the other in fulfilling its purposes.
4.__ Baptists believe it is proper for churches to be allowed tax funds to support their ministries.

(*Answers:* 1–F; 2–T; 3–T; 4–F)

The Baptist Faith & Message

Baptists and Religious Liberty

Baptists have always been the champions of religious liberty, not for themselves alone but for all men. The roots of modern Baptist churches are found in the Separatist movement in England and Holland. "In England among the early Baptists, both Thomas Helwys and John Murton advocated full religious liberty and paid for their stand in imprisonment and probably death. Helwys published in 1612 his *A Short Declaration of the Mystery of Iniquity* [addressed to the king], in which he upheld universal religious liberty, freedom of conscience for all, and declared that whether men be heretics, Turks, Jews, or whatever, the earthly power had no power to punish them for their views or to be intolerant of them."[3]

In America Roger Williams established the colony of Rhode Island with its charter calling for absolute religious liberty. Someone noted that for the first time since Constantine, a state existed in which religious liberty was expressly provided. The First Amendment to the United States Constitution was made largely upon the insistence of the Baptists of Virginia.

At the First Baptist World Congress in London in 1905, J. D. Freeman declared this position which is dear to the heart of every Baptist. "Our demand has been not simply for religious toleration, but religious liberty; not sufferance merely, but freedom; and that not for ourselves alone, but for all men. We did not stumble upon the doctrine. It inheres in the very essence of our belief. Christ is Lord of all. ... The conscience is the servant only of God, and is not subject to the will of man. This truth has indestructible life. Crucify it and the third day it will rise again. Bury it in the sepulchre and the stone will be rolled away, while the keepers become as dead men. ... Steadfastly refusing to bend our necks under the yoke of bondage, we have scrupulously withheld our hands from imposing that yoke upon others. ... Of martyr blood our hands are clean. We have never invoked the sword of temporal power to aid the sword of the Spirit. We have never passed an ordinance inflicting a civic disability on any man because of his religious views, be he Protestant or Papist, Jew, or Turk, or infidel. In this regard there is no blot on our escutcheon."[4]

If eternal vigilance is the price of freedom, it is especially true of religious liberty.

SOME QUESTIONS FOR FURTHER THOUGHT

1. What is the scriptural basis for religious liberty? How does the competency of the soul in religion relate to such liberty?

2. What matters are involved in Mullins' "religio-civic" axiom? What are their mutual responsibilities in the relationship between church and state? What things are forbidden in this relationship?

3. Should a church or any other religious body tell the state how to handle its affairs? How may individual Christians affect the political life of the country at various levels of government?

4. What should be the role of Baptists today in safeguarding religious liberty in America and in securing it throughout the world?

END NOTES

SECTION ONE: FOUNDATIONS OF THE FAITH

THE ROCK WHENCE WE ARE HEWN
1. E. Y. Mullins, *The Axioms of Religion* (Philadelphia: American Baptist Publication Society, 1908), 53.
2. *Ibid.*, 73-74.
3. See William L. Lumpkin, *Baptist Confessions of Faith.*
4. William L. Lumpkin, *Baptist Confessions of Faith* (Philadelphia: The Judson Press, 1959), 361.
5. Bill J. Leonard, *God's Last and Only Hope* (Philadelphia: Eerdmans, 1990), np.
6. *Ibid.*, 52-53.

THE SCRIPTURES
1. See William Barclay, *New Testament Words*; Herschel H. Hobbs, *Preaching Values from the Papyri.*
2. A. H. Strong, quoted by H. I. Hester, "Inspiration of the Scriptures," *Encyclopedia of Southern Baptists* (Nashville: Broadman Press, 1958), Vol. I, 686.
3. *Ibid.*
4. John P. Newport, "Authority of the Bible," *Encyclopedia of Southern Baptists* (Nashville: Broadman Press, 1958), Vol. I, 162.
5. Jack Finegan, *Light from the Ancient Past* (Princeton: Princeton University Press, 1959), 278.
6. See Jerry Vardaman, *Archaeology and the Living Word.*

SECTION TWO: BASIC TRUTHS OF THE FAITH

GOD
1. E. Y. Mullins, *The Christian Religion in Its Doctrinal Expression* (Nashville: Baptist Sunday School Board, 1917), 214-15.
2. *Ibid.*, 222-243.
3. See Hobbs, *An Exposition of the Gospel of Luke*, 33-43,48-56.
4. See Hobbs, *An Exposition of the Gospel of Matthew*, 413-418.

Man
1. W. T. Conner, *The Gospel of Redemption* (Nashville: Broadman Press, 1945), 6.

God's Purpose of Grace
1. E. Y. Mullins, *The Christian Religion in Its Doctrinal Expression* (Nashville: Baptist Sunday School Board, 1917), 347.

2. Frank Stagg, *New Testament Theology* (Nashville: Broadman Press, 1962), 88.

SECTION THREE: PEOPLE OF THE FAITH

The Church
    1. See Frank Stagg, *New Testament Theology*, 181. For an excellent treatment of the church see J. Clyde Turner, *The New Testament Doctrine of the Church.*
    2. To the 1925 Statement of "The Baptist Faith and Message" the 1963 Statement added "The New Testament speaks also of the church as the body of Christ which includes all of the redeemed of all the ages." A church history professor told the writer that this was the first new development in ecclesiology among Southern Baptists since 1845.
    3. For the writer's treatment of it, see *An Exposition of the Gospel of Matthew.*

Baptism and the Lord's Supper
    1. See Hobbs, *An Exposition of the Gospel of John*, 78-82.
    2. See Hobbs, *An Exposition of the Gospel of Mark*, 259-261.

The Lord's Day
    1. Frank Stagg, *New Testament Theology* (Nashville: Broadman Press, 1962), 296.

SECTION FIVE: PRACTICES OF THE FAITH

Education
    1. R. W. Weaver, as quoted by R. Orin Cornett, "Education, Southern Baptist," *Encyclopedia of Southern Baptists* (Nashville: Broadman Press, 1958), Vol. 1, 388.

Cooperation
    1. *Baptists of the World, 1905-1970* (Ft. Worth: Radio and Television Commission, 1970), 94.
    2. *Ibid.*

SECTION SIX: SOCIAL IMPLICATIONS OF THE FAITH

Peace and War
    1. Will and Ariel Durant, *The Lessons of History* (New York: Simon and Schuster, 1968), 81.

2. See Hobbs, *An Exposition of the Gospel of Luke*, 307-09.

3. E. Y. Mullins, *The Christian Religion and Its Doctrinal Expression* (Nashville: Baptist Sunday School Board, 1917), 427.

Religious Liberty

1. Eric Rust, "Religious Liberty," *Encyclopedia of Southern Baptists* (Nashville: Broadman Press, 1958), Vol II, 1153.

2. E. Y. Mullins, *The Axioms of Religion* (Philadelphia: American Baptist Publication Society, 1908), 72.

3. Rust, op. cit.

4. *Baptists of the World*, 1905-1970 (Ft. Worth: Radio and Television Commission, 1970), 91-92.

TEACHING GUIDE

THE BAPTIST FAITH
AND MESSAGE

TEACHING GUIDE FOR THE
BAPTIST FAITH AND MESSAGE

Mic Morrow

A study of *The Baptist Faith and Message* can be conducted in one of three ways. Consider which way best suits your church situation.

1. Individual approach. A person takes the responsibility for his or her learning by studying the book on a personal basis. By reading the text and answering the question(s) in the personal learning activities, an individual will gain knowledge about the biblical truths of the Christian faith. The advantage of this approach is that the individual can move at his or her own pace, set personal schedules, and select the time and place that best meet personalized needs. The disadvantage is the absence of group interaction.

Each chapter contains a personal learning activity. Paper and pencil will be needed for most of these activities.

2. Seminar approach. The seminar approach is primarily a leader-centered approach to learning. The seminar leader will guide an orderly presentation of each chapter using the lecture method as the primary method of teaching. This method would be appropriate if the pastor or other worship leader teaches the content in a worship service setting. Sunday and/or Wednesday evening services provide an avenue for using the seminar approach. Since the teaching guide is written for five one-hour sessions, the seminar leader would be wise to plan for additional time to include other facets of the worship service.

The lecture method can be supplemented with other methods to involve the participants. Reporting, question-and-answer, role-playing, discussion, use of overheads, and other methods are effective in getting the group involved in the learning process.

The study should be taught rather than preached. Seeking to involve the participants through problem-solving, case studies, and other methods will make for a more diversified and appealing time together. Although the teaching plan on the following pages is geared primarily to the small-group approach, the seminar leader can enhance his or her teaching by using some of the suggestions in the plan. Each participant should have a book.

3. Small-group approach. The small-group approach calls for a high degree of involvement by participants. The small-group study leader serves as teacher and facilitator for the group's interactive learning experiences. The session teaching plans provide blueprints for involving participants in the study through shared experiences and a variety of learning activities. Small-group settings, whether at church during Discipleship Training, in homes, or on retreats provide excellent opportunities for participants to experience intellectual, social, and spiritual growth.

This teaching guide is designed to enable the study leader to conduct five one-hour sessions without additional resources. However, for effective teaching the small-group study leader will need to do advance preparation for each of the five sessions. Such things as Bibles, tear sheets, masking tape, felt-tip markers, chalk, chalkboard, paper, and pencils will be needed for learning activities. Also, copies of suggested posters and worksheets will need to be made. Using overhead cels during the study sessions will enhance the learning atmosphere. Each participant should have a book.

Advance Preparation

Prior to the first session, several things should be done to ensure meaningful learning experiences for the participants. Do the following things well in advance of the sessions:

1. Order sufficient copies of *The Baptist Faith and Message*. Distribute these at least one week before the first session.

2. Publicize the study through verbal announcements, posters, personal mail, written announcements, and one-on-one invitations. Include the name of the teacher, schedule, place, and time with a brief description of the study content.

3. Study the entire text of the book, making a teaching outline. Complete the personal learning activities. Read the teaching guide and mark those activities that will require duplicating worksheets, making visual aids, and/or compiling teaching materials.

4. Read the Christian Growth Study Plan information in the back of the book. Plan how you will keep records of enrollment, participation, and application for Christian Growth Study Plan credit.

5. Make an overview poster giving each session goal and topics to be covered. (See page 149.)

Session Planning

Five sessions are suggested for teaching *The Baptist Faith and Message*. Be aware of how much time will be necessary to cover the material in each session. The teaching plans are guides and are flexible for individual situations.

Here are some suggestions for approaching each session:

1. Arrange the meeting room to create a learning atmosphere of expectation and anticipation. Setting up chairs so that participants can see the faces of one another is better than looking at the backs of heads. Create an interest center (a display related to the subject or a poster(s) on the wall).

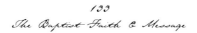

2. Have worksheets, visual aids, and teaching materials ready prior to the teaching time. At the end of this teaching plan are suggestions for posters and worksheets. The worksheets may be photocopied and enlarged for handout sheets and/or cels. The posters should be done on large sheets of paper or poster board.
3. Have on hand extra copies of *The Baptist Faith and Message* and the Bible.
4. Arrive early to greet all participants. Have a simple activity planned for early arrivers.
5. Begin promptly and end on time.
6. Be prepared to adjust and readjust for unforeseen circumstances.
7. Generate a feeling of enthusiasm about the study.
8. Pray at the beginning and end of each session.

Session 1

SECTION ONE: FOUNDATIONS OF THE FAITH

Session goal: As a result of studying Section One, members should be able to
- describe the foundation for Baptist beliefs; and
- state some basic beliefs about the Bible.

Before the Session

1. Display the overview poster.

2. Have copies of *The Baptist Faith and Message* on hand for those who do not have a copy. Ask someone to be responsible for registering participants.

3. Duplicate sufficient copies of the Baptist Faith and Message Matching Quiz (Listening Sheet) like the one on page 153. (The answers: 1-G, 2-F, 3-C, 4-I, 5-H, 6-A, 7-B, 8-J, 9-E, 10-D)

4. Have available several different translations of the Bible.

5. Prepare a Bible poster like the one on page 150.

During the Session

1. Begin with a prayer of commitment to Christ. Pray that as His church we will deepen our understanding of our beliefs.

2. Call attention to the overview poster. Read the goal for this session.

3. Comment on the meaning of Isaiah 51:1 as found on page 10 of *The Baptist Faith and Message*.

4. Give each person the Baptist Faith and Message Matching Quiz as a pretest of chapter 1. Tell participants to draw a line from the word(s) on the left to the correct definition on the right. Then use the quiz as a listening sheet as you teach the first chapter.

5. Write the words *doctrine* and *distinctive belief* on the chalkboard. Ask group members to state what they think of when they see these words. Lead the group to discuss reasons why doctrines or beliefs are important and why a study such as this is necessary. Identify the distinctive belief of "the competency of the soul in religion" and describe what it means.

6. Define other important terms listed on the Baptist Faith and Message Matching Quiz.

7. Refer the class to the six axioms of religion listed on page 12. Call on six persons to read one each and tell in his or her own words what the axiom means.

8. Present a lecture on the history of Baptist confessions of faith, including the development of the statement "The Baptist Faith and Message." Use the chalkboard to identify the dates for each. Conclude the lecture with an emphasis on the difference between a creed and a confession of faith.

9. Ask members to turn to the Preamble on page VI. Ask them to scan it. Call attention to the five considerations from the 1925 statement that were made a part of the report. Discuss the significance of these ideas. Point out that the final paragraph and sentence indicate the nature of the statement to be studied in the upcoming sessions.

10. Call for volunteers to use the Baptist Faith and Message Quiz (Listening Sheet) to recall brief definitions of words and terms in this chapter. Discuss the responses as a review of the chapter.

11. Introduce the chapter on the Scriptures by examining Hebrews 4:12. Read the verse from the *King James Version*. List some of the key words from the verse on the chalkboard (Word of God, quick, powerful, sharper, piercing, dividing asunder, joints and marrow, discerner of the thoughts and the intents of the heart).

Ask volunteers to suggest words that explain each word or phrase. Distribute the different Bible translations and ask participants to tell the different meanings of words in the verse. Write these beside the appropriate words. Here are some examples:

Word of God	God's message
quick	living; full of life; alive
powerful	active; energetic; effectual
sharper	more cutting; keener; cuts better
piercing	penetrating; strikes
dividing asunder	makes a distinction; severance
joints and marrow	inmost parts; innermost intimacies

| discerner of thoughts | able to judge the impulses; detecting the inmost thoughts; scrutinizing the very thought; exposes the very thoughts |
| intents of the heart | designs of the heart; purposes; motives |

Comment that God's Word is piercing and penetrating. God's Word cuts and lays everything open like a surgeon's scalpel. God can see into all corners of the soul, the life-principle of every person. He can see the spirit, the divine connection with God that sets man apart from all other living things. God's Word sits in judgment upon the thoughts (desires; the emotional side of life which is controlled by passions and feelings). (Intentions refers to the intellectual and volitional side of life.)

12. Examine basic beliefs about the Bible by calling on someone to read the statement about "The Scriptures" on page 19 of *The Baptist Faith and Message*. Comment that this is the basic belief of Baptists about the Bible. Give an overview of what the Scriptures are by defining several important words and concepts:

(1) *Biblos*—Greek word for the inner bark of papyrus reed; dried and woven together the *biblos* could be written on; eventually the word came to mean "book."

(2) *Inspired*—"breathed in"; the Bible is called the inspired Word of God because God "breathed in" to the minds of the writers. Call on volunteers to read 2 Timothy 3:16–17 and 2 Peter 1:21. Comment that about 40 writers felt inspired to put their ideas, visions, concepts, and feelings into words over thousands of years.

Explain the meaning of the four theories of inspiration—intuition, illumination, dictation, and dynamical. (Use the information on pages 20–21 of *The Baptist Faith and Message*.)

(3) A *book of religion*—Emphasize the main content of the section, "A Book of Religion" on page 24.

(4) *Authoritative*—Explain what is meant by authoritative by using the content of "An Authoritative Book" on page 25.

(5) *It is living and active*—The Word of God is more than print on a page (read Isa. 55:11). It gives life (read Ps. 119:105; 19:7; Prov. 6:23; and 2 Cor. 3:6).

(6) *Its makeup*:
- It is a collection of many books in one volume.
- It is divided into two main sections: the Old Testament of 39 books (Law–5; History–12; Poetry–5; Major Prophets–5; Minor Prophets–12); the New Testament of 27 books (Biography–4; History–1; Paul's Letters–13; General Letters–8; Prophecy–1).

- "Testament" in referring to the Bible means "covenant." Old Testament (Old Covenant)—God's agreement with Abraham and his people; New Testament (New Covenant)—God's agreement with anyone who will accept Christ as Lord and Savior.
  - Old Testament was written in Hebrew; New Testament was written in Greek.

(7) *Holy* means set aside for a special purpose.

13. Display the Bible poster. Read each statement aloud and comment briefly as a review of this chapter.

Ask each person to complete this statement:

"To me the Bible is _____." Discuss the reasons for their answers.

14. Close with a prayer of thanksgiving for God's Word and what it is doing to change lives.

Session 2
SECTION TWO: BASIC TRUTHS OF THE FAITH

Session goal: As a result of studying Section Two, members should be able to state in their own words at least two basic Bible teachings about (1) God as Father, Son, and Holy Spirit, (2) man, (3) salvation, and (4) grace.

Before the Session

1. Display the overview poster.

2. Make 14 Scripture slips with assignments to look up selected verses identifying God. Use the worksheet master on page 154.

3. Have three poster sheets (write *Father* at the top of one, *Son* at the top of one, and *Holy Spirit* at the top of one) and three felt-tip markers available.

4. Enlist six persons to read selected Scripture verses on election—Romans 9:11; Romans 11:5; Romans 11:7; Romans 11:28; 1 Thessalonians 1:4; and 2 Peter 1:10.

5. Make a poster listing facts on the security of the believer (see master poster on page 150).

During the Session

1. Read the session goal from the overview poster. Pray asking God's guidance in achieving the goal.

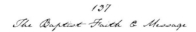

2. Examine individual feelings and thoughts about God. Divide the class into groups of four persons and ask each group member to individually answer the question: When did God become more than just a word to you? Reassemble the group. Call for volunteers to tell what somebody else in his or her small group said about God.

3. Give a brief testimony of your relationship with God and how you have come to see different aspects of Him as you have grown in your Christian life.

4. Explain the meaning of *Elohim, Adonai,* and *Yahweh.* Examine one focus Scripture verse—Exodus 3:14 by reading the verse from the Bible. Explain the context of the verse. Explain the meaning of the verse by giving the basic meaning of Yahweh—"He causes to be," or "He is," or "He will be," or "I cause to be what comes into existence." The phrase "I AM" also means "I will be what(ever) I will be" which underscores the continuing revelation of Yahweh.

5. Comment that God is too great to be confined by words, but we have to use words to try to explain who He is. Ask for personal expressions people give in explaining who God is. Write these expressions on the chalkboard.

6. Explore terms from the Bible that refer to God by handing out the 14 Scripture slips to individuals or teams. Ask group members to use the verses to read about terms that refer to God and to tell what the terms are. Clarify the terms, if necessary .(Master Worksheet #2).

7. Examine the seven natural and four moral attributes of God that are dis-cussed on pages 32–33. (self-existence, immutability, omnipresence, immen-sity, eternity, omniscience, omnipotence, holiness, righteousness, truth, and love) by assigning one each of the attributes to different group members. Ask each member to read from the book the explanation of his or her attribute and comment briefly on it.

8. Divide the group into three small groups. Give each group a sheet of poster paper and a felt-tip marker. Assign each small group one of the three relationships God has with man (Father, Son, Holy Spirit). Ask them to read the information in the book and to write at least four words or statements to give understanding to the particular relationship. After several minutes, call for reports.

9. Comment that man has many of the attributes of God, but that he lacks many also. Man was created in the image of God which indicates that he has the potential to use those given attributes in the way God would.

10. In a general discussion examine individual feelings and thoughts about man by asking for true or false responses to the following statements:
   a. Genesis teaches that the creation of man is no more special than the creation of all other forms of life. (*False.* Man was the climax of God's creative work; man was the goal of God's work in creation.)
   b. The Bible teaches that man consists of a unity—a total being. (*True.* Man is both spirit and body. He is a soul who possesses a body.)

c. Man's distinctiveness is that he is created in God's image. (*True. Man has a spiritual nature.*)

11. Relate the story of the fall of man by identifying how man yielded to the temptation to sin. Compare the three general areas of temptation Adam and Eve experienced in the garden of Eden to the ones Jesus experienced in the wilderness.

12. Ask, What separated man from God and what brings him back to God? Without saying anything, write the word "SIN" in capital letters on the chalkboard. Across the word "SIN" draw a picture of the cross. Call on someone to explain the image you have drawn. (Answer: Christ's death on the cross conquered sin and allows man an opportunity to have a right relationship with the Father.)

13. Examine basic beliefs about man by calling on six persons to read one of the six sentences on page 43 of *The Baptist Faith and Message* under "Man." After each sentence is read, ask volunteers to tell what the sentence means. When all the sentences and meanings have been given, ask someone to summarize his or her personal belief about man.

14. Focus on the subjects of sin and salvation by commenting that salvation cannot be understood until a person understands sin.

15. Give one each of the following Scripture references to eight individuals to read. Ask each to define sin, according to the Scripture passage assigned.

(a) Genesis 6:5   (e) Romans 3:10–23
(b) Psalm 51:4   (f) Galatians 5:19–21
(c) Jeremiah 17:9   (g) James 4:17
(d) John 16:8–9   (h) 1 John 3:4

Explanations should be similar to the following: Sin is basically rebellion against God. Sin leads man to make himself the center of his universe. Sin involves the nature of man and includes thoughts and emotions, as well as acts of disobedience.

16. Write the word law on the chalkboard. Beside it write the word Jesus. Draw an x over the word law and comment that man could not be saved by the law. Draw a circle around the word *Jesus* and comment that salvation by grace through faith in Jesus Christ is the only way.

17. Examine basic Baptist beliefs about salvation by looking at three aspects—regeneration, sanctification, and glorification. Lecture on each term using the information in chapter 5.

18. Focus on the subject of *grace* by reading the definition of grace. Grace is the undeserved favor of God toward man in spite of what man has done against God.

19. Examine basic Baptist beliefs about grace by reading aloud the first paragraph of "God's Purpose of Grace" on page 55 of *The Baptist Faith and Message*. Lead a discussion of "Election" using the material on pages 55–58.

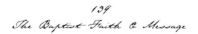

Call on the six persons enlisted before the session to read the assigned Scripture verses on election—Romans 9:11; Romans 11:5; Romans 11:7; Romans 11:28; 1 Thessalonians 1:4; 2 Peter 1:10. Comment that "election" is a mystery; no one can fully explain it. Ask, What is your concept of election? Discuss answers. Conclude any discussion on the doctrine of election by commenting that God is not limited by time. With God there is no present, past, and future, but one eternal now. He knows all things from the beginning. Thus God's election does not nullify man's freedom of choice. God knows what man's choice will be.

20. Read aloud the second paragraph of "God's Purpose of Grace" on page 55 of *The Baptist Faith and Message*. (Use the information on the subtopic "Perseverance" on pages 58–60 as support.) Examine reasons why Christians cannot "fall from grace." Display the poster listing facts on the security of the believer. (See master poster on page 150.)

Call on volunteers to read at least one Scripture per statement and to tell their personal interpretations of the statements.

21. Examine the subtopic "The Christian and Sin" by emphasizing that the love of God is so great that He forgives our sins. Look at various verses of Scripture that deal with the Christian and sin. Read the verses aloud and explain them based on the information in the subtopic.

22. Conclude with a prayer of praise for God's great gift of salvation through His Son.

SECTION THREE: PEOPLE OF THE FAITH
SECTION FOUR: FULFILLMENT OF THE FAITH

Session goal: As a result of studying Sections Three and Four, members should be able to define the church and give at least two biblical truths about the church, explain the meaning of the two ordinances Baptists observe and the purpose of setting the Lord's Day aside as a special day, understand the meaning of the kingdom of God and specific words related to end times.

Before the Session

1. Display the overview poster.
2. Enlist two persons for a role-playing situation as described below.
3. Make a poster—"I will build MY church."
4. Make four statement strips for display.
5. Make two placards—*eschatology* and *Parousia*.

During the Session

1. Call attention to the session goal. In the opening prayer, ask for God's leadership in attaining the goal.

2. Introduce the subject of the church by presenting the role-playing situation. Set the scene of two friends talking together. One person is active in the church and wants the other person to attend. The other person is not involved in the church and does not see the importance of the church. The active person should give good reasons a person should be involved in church. The inactive person should give excuses for not attending church.

Divide the class into two listening groups. Group 1 should listen for the good reasons for attending church. Group 2 should listen for the excuses used for not attending church. After each person has presented reasons and excuses, stop the action. Call on volunteers from group 1 to tell the reasons they heard. Call on volunteers from group 2 to tell the excuses they heard. Discuss reasons why Christians should be involved in the church.

3. Write the following words on the chalkboard—*ekklesia*, *petros*, and *petra*. Using the material in the two subtopics "Significance of the Word" and "Jesus and the Church," clarify the meaning of church and its foundation. Display the poster—"I will build MY church."

4. As you explain the mission of the church using the subtopic "Mission of the Church," call on several volunteers to read the appropriate Scripture verses.

5. Speak briefly on "The Church and the Kingdom." Emphasize that the church is one phase of the kingdom.

6. Write the word *officers* on the chalkboard. Read Philippians 1:1. Explain that the word *bishop* also is translated as *pastor, overseer, minister of the church, superintendent,* and *elder.* Refer to the material under "Officers of the Local Church." Explain that the word *deacon* also is translated as *minister* and *assistant.*

7. Write the word *autonomous* on the chalkboard. Explain that autonomous means that each church is only under the lordship of Christ. Baptist churches do not have a ruling body that tells them what to do. Each church uses the democratic process to make decisions. Each member has an equal vote. Ask, What problems could occur in this process? Allow time for responses.

8. Introduce the subject of the ordinances as you divide the group into two subgroups. Assign Group 1 the subject of baptism and Group 2 the subject of the Lord's Supper. Ask each subgroup to read the assigned subtopic silently and to mark important words in each paragraph. After sufficient time appoint a leader in each subgroup to guide a discussion of the subtopic using the key words. Call the subgroups together. Ask the subgroup leaders to report on the discussions in their groups.

9. Introduce the subject of the Lord's Day by reading the initial statement about the Lord's Day on page 79. Display the four statement strips as you read.

10. Examine the meaning of the Lord's Day by giving an understanding of *Sabbath.* Explain that the root means "to cease, desist." The idea is not of relaxation or refreshment, but cessation from activity. It originated as a way to provide rest from the burden of labor. It came to mean "rest."

Tell about the New Testament concepts of the Sabbath.

(1) The Pharisees followed a hard and fast rule for Sabbath observance;
(2) Jesus evidently was not as strict in following the letter of the law. Call on volunteers to read Matthew 12:9–12 and John 5:5–16. Explain the Scripture verses.
(3) The disciples evidently did not hold hard and fast to Sabbath observance. Read Matthew 12:1; Mark 2:23; and Luke 6:1. Explain each verse.

Review Chapter 9 by reading and answering the questions at the end of the chapter.

11. Introduce the subject of the Kingdom by emphasizing this statement: "Particularly the Kingdom is the realm of salvation into which men enter by trustful, childlike commitment to Jesus Christ." Use the three subtopics in the chapter to clarify what the kingdom of God is.

12. Examine the meaning of "Last Things" by highlighting some key points

on the doctrine of last things. Display the two placards *eschatology* and *Parousia*. Define *eschatology*—view of last or final things. Define *Parousia*—Greek word referring to the coming of Christ.

Lecture on Jesus' teachings regarding His return and the end of the age.

Conclude this session by talking about the imminency of Christ's return. Offer a prayer for the group that as Christians we will always be ready for Christ's return.

Session 4
SECTION FIVE: PRACTICES OF THE FAITH

Session goal: As a result of studying Section Five, members should be able to express their basic belief about evangelism and missions, education, stewardship, and cooperation.

Before the Session

1. Display the overview poster.

2. Make a Scripture poster strip using the first part of Matthew 28:19 from the *New International Version*.

During the Session

1. Call on two persons to begin the session—one to read the goal for this session and the other to voice a prayer.

2. Introduce this session by indicating that evangelism and missions, education, stewardship, and cooperation are elements of a church's need to work together to fulfill God's will.

3. Emphasize that evangelism and missions should be the top priority in every Christians' desire to bring glory to God. Examine the meaning of "Evangelism and Missions" by reading the statement from *The Baptist Faith and Message* on "Evangelism and Missions" on page 94. Clarify the statement by referring to the Great Commission (Matt. 28:18–20) as the basis of evangelism and missions. Display the Scripture poster strip of Matthew 28:19. Comment that a better interpretation of "go" is *as you go*. Emphasize that the most important part of the Great Commission is to "make disciples." Stress the idea that the Great Commission was given to the church (Eph. 3:9–11).

Ask, How do we make disciples? Allow several persons to respond.

Read aloud the subtopic "Life of the Church" on page 95. Ask volunteers to tell of any personal involvement in mission activities. Briefly explain the church's program of evangelism and missions.

4. Examine the doctrine of education by exploring Scripture related to education. Assign each person to read Deuteronomy 6:1–9. Ask each one to identify words or phrases that relate to teaching. Call for responses. List these on the chalkboard.

Instruct each person to read 2 Timothy 3:14–17. Ask the question, What do the verses say about learning? Call for responses.

Quote Matthew 5:2 and explain that the Sermon on the Mount was a time of teaching Jesus had with His followers.

Say: Jesus was called "teacher" (*rabbi, rabboni*) by His followers. He was known far and wide by friends and foes as a teacher. "Rabbi, we know you are a teacher who has come from God" (John 3:2, NIV).

Assign selected persons to read verses of Scripture that deal with teaching.

(1) 1 Samuel 12:23   (4) Luke 11:1
(2) Psalm 32:8   (5) 1 Timothy 3:2
(3) Psalm 143:10   (6) James 3:1

Comment briefly on each verse.

Stress the importance the Bible places on teaching. Emphasize that the church is obligated to teach. Explore the Southern Baptist view of education. Call on someone to read the first paragraph under "Education" on page 97 of *The Baptist Faith and Message*. Comment that since "to educate" is one of the purposes of the church, the church should endeavor to promote education.

Call on someone to read the second paragraph under "Education" on page 97 of *The Baptist Faith and Message*. Based on this paragraph, call for opinions on the following statements.

(1) A teacher should have the freedom to teach his or her personal beliefs in a Baptist school even if those beliefs are contrary to what most Baptists believe.

(2) A Christian teacher who teaches a course on a non-religious subject (math, chemistry, biology, etc.) should not bring "religion" into the classroom.

5. Examine the doctrine of stewardship by exploring Scripture related to stewardship. Comment that the word *tithe* means 10 percent. Assign one of the following Scripture passages to each of three small groups.

(1) Leviticus 27:30–32
(2) Deuteronomy 8:18
(3) Malachi 3:8–12

Call for brief interpretations.

Ask, What did Jesus teach about stewardship? Suggest that answers can be found in these passages.

(1) Matthew 6:1–4
(2) Matthew 6:19–21

(3) Matthew 19:16–22

(4) Matthew 23:23

(5) Matthew 25:14–30

(6) Luke 12:16–31

(7) Luke 16:1–13

Ask participants to look up the passages and be prepared to tell Jesus' teaching about stewardship.

Explore Southern Baptist teachings on stewardship by reading aloud the statement on "Stewardship" on page 101 of *The Baptist Faith and Message*.

Assign each of the three small groups a different subtopic in the chapter. Tell each group to read and discuss the subtopic, and then present an overview of the content.

Explain that stewardship involves much more than money, but that money is one of the tangible expressions of our commitment to Christ. Express that stewardship of our time is very important. Ask group members to ponder this thought: If a Christian gave 10 percent of his or her time to do the Lord's work, what differences would be seen in the church and in the community? Call for responses.

6. Examine the doctrine of cooperation by exploring Scripture related to cooperation. Look at several incidents of cooperation by groups or individuals in the New Testament by asking volunteers to read and tell about the following.

(1) Matthew 10:1–13

(2) Mark 2:1–5

(3) Luke 10:1–9

(4) Acts 4:31–37

There is ample evidence that the churches of the New Testament cooperated with each other. For example, Acts 15 and Galatians 2 are about the Jerusalem conference meeting with regard to doctrinal purity. Representatives of the churches at Jerusalem and Antioch met to confer about the Judaizer controversy. The result: Both churches agreed to a gospel of salvation by grace through faith as opposed to a message of works plus faith.

Also, First Corinthians 16:1-4 and Second Corinthians 8—9 are about the churches of Macedonia and Greece making an offering for the relief of suffering Jewish Christians in Palestine.

Explore the Southern Baptist concept of cooperation by asking participants to read silently the initial statement on "Cooperation" on page 106 of *The Baptist Faith and Message*. Clarify the statement by lecturing on the material in the chapter.

7. Close with a prayer thanking God for our denomination and its plans to evangelize the lost throughout the world.

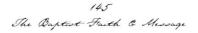

Session 5

SECTION SIX: SOCIAL
IMPLICATIONS OF THE FAITH

Session goal: As a result of studying Section Six, members should be able to state what they believe about the Christian and the social order, peace and war, and religious liberty.

Before the Session

1. Display the overview poster.

2. Make ample copies of the fill-in-the-blanks Scripture quiz on the Christian and the social order like the one on page 155 (Master Worksheet #3). The answers are:

(1) good; require; justly

(2) truth; truth and peace

(3) light; good works

(4) love thy neighbour as thyself

(5) hungred; thirsty; ye took me in

3. Collect two sheets of poster paper, felt-tip markers, and masking tape. Write *Separation of Church and State* at the top of one paper and *Baptists and Religious Freedom* at the top of the other.

During the Session

1. Lead in a prayer of commitment to God's leadership in His work through Southern Baptist churches.

2. Read the session goal from the displayed overview poster.

3. Examine the doctrine of the Christian and the social order through an exploration of Scripture related to the Christian and the social order. Give each person a fill-in-the-blanks Scripture quiz and ask each to fill in the blanks. Ask volunteers to read the verses with the correct words and to tell what the verses say about relationships with humankind. Ask, What are practical implications of each verse? Allow several persons to respond.

Explore Southern Baptist views on the Christian and the social order by reading aloud "The Christian and the Social Order" on page 112 of *The Baptist Faith and Message.*

Divide the class into five small groups. Assign one each of the subtopics in chapter 16—(1) Introduction (first paragraph); (2) Personal Regeneration Basic; (3) The Christian and Society; (4) Christian Citizenship; and (5) Social Cooperation. Ask each group to prepare and present a subtopic synopsis.

4. Examine the doctrine of peace and war by looking at several Scripture verses related to peace and war. Write the words *Peace* and *War* on the chalkboard. Around these two words write these Scripture references: Isaiah 2:4; Matthew 5:9; Matthew 5:38–48; Matthew 6:33; Matthew 26:52; Romans 12:18–19; Romans 14:19; Hebrews 12:14; and James 4:1–2. With a piece of chalk draw a large X through the word *War*. Comment that the gospel of Christ is one of peace, not war. War is a result of man's greed and selfishness.

Ask each participant to read silently one selected Scripture reference. Call for volunteers to paraphrase each verse.

Explore Southern Baptist views on peace and war by reading aloud the statement on "Peace and War" on page 116 of *The Baptist Faith and Message.* Tell each person to find the answers in chapter 17 as you ask the following questions.

(1) From the introduction—How many years of peace have there been in the last 3,421 years of recorded history? (268 years)

(2) From "Prophecy or Condition?"—When will there be peace on earth? (Not until there is glory to God in the highest, as men through faith in His Son submit to His will.)

(3) From "Prophecy or Condition?"—According to James 4:1–3, there will be war as long as what is in the human heart? (lust)

(4) From "Prophecy or Condition?"—What must precede reconciliation of man to man? (Reconciliation of man to God)

(5) From "Jesus and War"—According to 2 Corinthians 5:17–21 and Ephesians 2:13–17, why did Jesus give His life? (That He might establish the grounds for peace between God and man and between man and man.);

—What leads us to believe that although Jesus abhorred war, He did teach the right of defending one's person, home, and nation? (See subtopic, "Jesus and War," p. 117. For defensive purposes, Jesus seems to have permitted the use of a sword.)

(6) From "The Christian and War"—As a Christian citizen of a state, what does good citizenship require if a person's nation is threatened by aggression? (That one defend his nation)

(7) From "The Christian and Peace"—What is the true remedy for the war spirit? (The gospel of Christ)

5. Examine the doctrine of religious liberty by defining religious liberty and exploring Scripture verses related to religious liberty. Call on a volunteer to read the subtopic "Definition of Religious Liberty." Call on volunteers to read Romans 6:6–18 and Galatians 5:13–16. Ask, What do these two Scripture passages say about religious liberty? Allow several persons to respond.

Read "Scriptural Basis of Religious Liberty." At each Scripture reference, call on someone to read the verse(s). Ask for other Scripture verses that deal with religious liberty.

Explore the Southern Baptist view of the doctrine of religious liberty by attaching to the wall two sheets of poster paper. Write the words *Separation of Church and State* on one and *Baptists and Religious Liberty* on the other. Divide the class into two groups. Assign one group to read "Separation of Church and State," and write on the poster paper a brief outline of the content. Ask the other group to read "Baptists and Religious Liberty" and to write on the poster paper a brief outline of the content. Call for reports from each group.

6. If time permits, give a brief review of the 18 doctrines covered in this study. Call on volunteers to tell some things they have learned during the study.

7. Conclude with a prayer of commitment to live a life of Christian principles in a world of non-Christian principles.

THE BIBLE

- The inspired and authoritative record of God's revelation of Himself to humankind
- Written by persons divinely inspired
- Final authority about all matters of faith and moral duty
- Christ and His gift of salvation are its main teachings

Master Poster # 2

THE SECURITY OF THE BELIEVER
(The Perseverance of the Saints)

1. God promises and gives eternal life.
   John 3:16,18,36; 5:24; 6:47; 1 John 2:25; Titus 1:2

2. The believer has everlasting life.
   John 3:18,36; 5:24; 6:47; 10:27–28; 1 John 5:13

3. Christians do not keep themselves.
   1 Peter 1:3–6; Jude 24—25; John 10:28

4. The Christian is hidden with Christ in God.
   Colossians 3:3

5. We are born the children of God, and we cannot be unborn.
   John 3:5

6. Nothing can separate us from the love of God.
   Romans 8:35–39

7. When God's children sin, He chastises them and keeps them.
   Psalm 89:30–36

8. Sins of Christians are not charged to them, so they do not have to die for them.
   Romans 4:7–8

Master Poster # 3

"I WILL BUILD MY CHURCH."

Master Poster # 4

STATEMENTS:

- Should be employed in exercises of worship and spiritual devotion, both public and private.

- By refraining from worldly amusements.

- Resting from secular employments.

- Work of necessity and mercy only being excepted.

Master Poster # 5

"Therefore go and make disciples"
(Matt. 28:19, NIV).

Master Poster # 6

PLACARDS:

Eschatology

Parousia

Master Poster # 7

BAPTIST FAITH AND MESSAGE MATCHING QUIZ

(Listening Sheet)

1. doctrines

a. book of the Jewish/Christian faith revealing God's interaction with humankind

2. competency

b. the whole body of Christians; a place of public worship

3. non-creedal

c. opposed to an authoritarian formula of religious belief

4. priesthood

d. ordinances for remembering Christ's death and symbolizing His death, burial, and resurrection

5. regenerated

e. self-governing and rule by the majority of the members

6. Bible

f. sufficiency, right, ability

7. church

g. beliefs and/or principles accepted by a body of believers

8. Great Commission

h. reformed; changed radically for the better

9. autonomy and democracy

i. the character, dignity, and office of one who has direct access to God

10. Lord's Supper and baptism

j. Christ's command for His followers to teach and baptize

SCRIPTURE VERSES
IDENTIFYING GOD

Cut these slips apart and give one each to 14 persons or teams. Ask an assigned person to read the verse and identify a word or phrase identifying God.

1. Ecclesiastes 12:1 (Creator)

2. Genesis 15:1 (Shield, reward)

3. Deuteronomy 33:27 (Refuge)

4. Deuteronomy 32:4 (Rock)

5. Psalm 27:1 (Light, salvation, strength)

6. Psalm 31:3 (Rock, fortress)

7. Psalm 7:17 (Most high)

8. Psalm 46:1 (Refuge, strength, help)

9. Mark 14:36 (Father)

10. Psalm 7:8 (Judge)

11. Nahum 1:7 (Good, a stronghold)

12. John 4:24 (Spirit)

13. Exodus 6:3 (Jehovah)

14. 2 Samuel 22:2 (Rock, fortress, deliverer)

Master Worksheet # 2

SCRIPTURE QUIZ

Fill in the missing words in the following Scripture verses.

1. He hath shewed thee, O man, what is_____ ; and
   what doth the Lord _____ of thee,
   but to do _____ , and to love mercy, and to walk
   humbly with thy God? (Mic. 6:8).

2. These are the things that ye shall do; Speak ye every man the
   _____ to his neighbour;
   execute the judgment of _____ in your gates
   (Zech. 8:16).

3. Let your _____ so shine before men, that they
   may see your _____ , and
   glorify your Father which is in heaven (Matt. 5:16).

4. And the second is like unto it, Thou shalt _____
   _____(Matt. 22:39).

5. For I was an _____ , and ye gave me meat: I was
   _____, and ye gave me drink:
   I was a stranger, and _____ (Matt. 25:35).

BIBLIOGRAPHY

To order *The Baptist Faith and Message* tract (item 0-6330-0302-6), write to LifeWay Church Resources Customer Service; One LifeWay Plaza; Nashville, TN 37234-0113; phone toll free (800) 458-2772; fax order to (615) 251-5933; order online at *www.lifeway.com*; or order from a state Baptist convention office.

Barclay, William. *New Testament Words*. Naperville, Illinois: Alec R. Allenson, Inc., 1964.

Criswell W. A. *Expository Sermons on the Book of Daniel*. Vol. 1. Grand Rapids: Zondervan, 1968.

Hobbs, Herschel H. *An Exposition of the Gospel of John*. Grand Rapids: Baker, 1968.

———. *An Exposition of the Gospel of Luke*. Grand Rapids: Baker, 1966.

———. *An Exposition of the Gospel of Mark*. Grand Rapids: Baker, n.d.

———. *An Exposition of the Gospel of Matthew*. Grand Rapids: Baker, 1965.

———. *Preaching Values from the Papyri*. Grand Rapids: Baker, 1964.

Lumpkin, William L. *Baptist Confessions of Faith*. Philadelphia: The Judson Press, 1959.

Turner, J. Clyde. *The New Testament Doctrine of the Church*. Nashville: Broadman Press, 1951.

Vardaman, Jerry. *Archaeology and the Living Word*. Nashville: Broadman Press, 1965.

CHRISTIAN
GR🌐WTH
STUDY PLAN

In the **Christian Growth Study Plan (formerly Church Study Course)**, this book *The Baptist Faith and Message* is a resource for course credit in the subject area Baptist Doctrine of the Christian Growth category of plans. To receive credit, read the book, complete the learning activities, show your work to your pastor, a staff member or church leader, then complete the information on the next page. The form may be duplicated. Send the completed page to:

Christian Growth Study Plan
One LifeWay Plaza
Nashville, TN 37234-0117
FAX: (615)251-5067
Email: cgspnet@lifeway.com

For information about the Christian Growth Study Plan, refer to the Christian Growth Study Plan Catalog. It is located online at www.lifeway.com/cgsp. If you do not have access to the Internet, contact the Christian Growth Study Plan office (1.800.968.5519) for the specific plan you need for your ministry.

THE BAPTIST FAITH AND MESSAGE
COURSE NUMBER: CG-0149

PARTICIPANT INFORMATION

Social Security Number (USA ONLY-optional)
– –

Personal CGSP Number*
–

Date of Birth (MONTH, DAY, YEAR)
– –

Name (First, Middle, Last)

Home Phone
–

Address (Street, Route, or P.O. Box)

City, State, or Province

Zip/Postal Code

Please check appropriate box: ☐ Resource purchased by self ☐ Resource purchased by church ☐ Other

CHURCH INFORMATION

Church Name

Address (Street, Route, or P.O. Box)

City, State, or Province

Zip/Postal Code

CHANGE REQUEST ONLY

☐ Former Name

☐ Former Address

City, State, or Province

Zip/Postal Code

☐ Former Church

City, State, or Province

Zip/Postal Code

Signature of Pastor, Conference Leader, or Other Church Leader

Date

*New participants are requested but not required to give SS# and date of birth. Existing participants, please give CGSP# when using SS# for the first time. Thereafter, only one ID# is required. **Mail to:** Christian Growth Study Plan, One LifeWay Plaza, Nashville, TN 37234-0117. Fax: (615)251-5067.

Rev. 3-03

The Light Still Shines

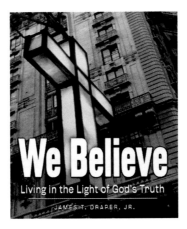

In this age of spiritual darkness a battle rages that has eternal consequences for every person on earth. It is a battle for the truth.

Many people determine truth according to a particular religious system. Some claim that absolute truth does not exist—truth is relative. Still others live by a hodgepodge of ideas gathered from popular culture.

Christians know that absolute truth exists, and it is found in God's Word. *We Believe* gives you a biblical belief system that equips you to answer the important questions in life:
- What is God like, and how do we know?
- Who are we, and how can we know God personally?
- Why did God establish the church, and what is our role in it?
- What is our purpose in life?
- Should Christians try to shape society?
- Where is this world headed?
- How can we participate in God's plan?

Ultimate truth is a person. Jesus Christ is the Light of the world who shows us the way.

WE BELIEVE
JAMES T. DRAPER JR.
ISBN 0-6330-9129-4

Order by writing to LifeWay Church Resources Customer Service; One LifeWay Plaza; Nashville, TN 37234-0113; faxing (615) 251-5933; phoning toll free (800) 458-2772; ordering online at *www.lifeway.com*; or visiting a LifeWay Christian Store.

OVERVIEW POSTER

Session 1 (Section One)

Goal: As a result of studying this section, participants should be able to (1) describe the foundation for Baptist beliefs and (2) state some basic beliefs about the Bible.

Topics: The Rock Whence We Are Hewn, and The Scriptures

Session 2 (Section Two)

Goal: As a result of studying this section, participants should be able to state in his or her own words at least two basic Bible teachings about (1) God as Father, Son, and Holy Spirit, (2) man, (3) salvation, and (4) grace.

Topics: God, Man, Salvation, and God's Purpose of Grace

Session 3 (Sections Three and Four)

Goal: As a result of studying these sections, members should be able to define the church and give at least two biblical truths about the church, explain the meaning of the two ordinances Baptists observe and the purpose of setting the Lord's Day aside as a special day, understand the meaning of the kingdom of God and specific words related to end times.

Topics: The Church, Baptism and the Lord's Supper, The Lord's Day, The Kingdom, and Last Things

Session 4 (Section Five)

Goal: As a result of studying this section, participants should be able to express their basic belief about evangelism and missions, education, stewardship, and cooperation.

Topics: Evangelism and Missions, Education, Stewardship, and Cooperation

Session 5 (Section Six)

Goal: As a result of studying this section, participants should be able to state what they believe about the Christian and the social order, peace and war, and religious liberty.

Topics: The Christian and the Social Order, Peace and War, and Religious Liberty

Master Poster # 1